SEDUCTIVE
TABLES FOR TWO

TABLESCAPES, PICNICS, & RECIPES THAT INSPIRE ROMANCE

MOLL ANDERSON PRODUCTIONS

SEDUCTIVE
TABLES FOR TWO

TABLESCAPES, PICNICS, & RECIPES THAT INSPIRE ROMANCE

MOLL ANDERSON

First published in the United States of America in 2012 by Moll Anderson Productions.
265 Brookview Town Centre Way, Suite 501, Knoxville, Tennessee 37919

Printed in Italy
10 9 8 7 6 5 4 3 2 1

EAN: 978-1-937268-03-9

Cover & Interior Design: Sheri Ferguson, Ferguson Design Studio,
   and Moll Anderson, Moll Anderson Productions

Publisher/Managing Editor: Cindy Games, Moll Anderson Productions

Copyeditor: Lisa Grimenstein

Interior Design & Photo Styling: Moll Anderson, Moll Anderson Productions

Photo Styling & Pre-production Assistant: Ashley Cate, Moll Anderson Productions

Cover Photography: Mark DeLong, DeLong Photography

Hair & Makeup: Brady Wardlaw

Recipes edited and tested by Nicki Pendleton Wood with Meg Giuffrida

www.mollanderson.com

EXTRA SPECIAL THANKS

To my amazing husband, Charlie Anderson—my best friend, partner, and mentor. I love you and I love our life together! You continually inspire me to create. Laters, baby.

To my son, Michael, I'm so proud of you, your heart, your spirit of entrepreneurship, and for wanting to be on my team and supporting my dream. Aphrodite, my daughter (-in-law), you are truly a joy; you are talented, fun to work beside, and a fab wife to my son! Hayley, Aaron, and our granddaughter Gracie Elizabeth, Chase and Lauren—you are all amazing to watch as you take on the world. I'm so proud to be your stepmom and GiGi.

To my mother-in-law and father-in-law—Hilda and Charles Anderson Sr.—thank you for your love and support. To all my family—the Ruffalos, the Keaggys, and the Andersons. Sis, Susan Anderson, I'm so grateful for our Saturdays together. To Karen Sue, my bestie, who defies aging: here's to stolen moments! John Hall—your magnificent photography, talent, and eye. To my childhood girlfriends, Missy Anderson and Jinger Richardson, for their wonderful love and support. Nancy Lacy—let's have a cinnamon roll. Penny, my sister-friend, congrats for making Lindsay's Dream a reality. Dee Haslam, thank you again for your support and RIVR Media time and time again. Cristina Ferrare, you are my soul sister! Kitty Moon Emery, who still believes in me and I know is always there. Mrs. Stacie Standifer Nichols, it all started with *Nashville Lifestyles* magazine, baby! Stephanie Hanson, an angel who hangs out and watches over "Mary Ellen Kay."

To "Team Moll": Cindy Games, Vice President and Publisher of Moll Anderson Productions, oh my gosh—our 3rd book together and counting; I couldn't do it without you! Linda Willey, Executive Director of the Charlie and Moll Anderson Family Foundation, thanks for all the chicken soup and laughter. Ashley Cate, creative coordinator, you should be Louboutin at the very least. Sheri Ferguson, graphic designer extraordinaire; Pat Adair—"Pat O" you are the rock; Britta Bollinger, flower child; Elder Carrillo, you're the best; Marilyn Spears, aka Sophie's other mom, and winner of the house style award. To Brady Wardlaw, my bud who can whip up my hair and make me look seductive all while holding a martini in his hand. To Karen Hosack, who is truly a rock star! Loretta Cate, my "REAL" housewife. Paulette Kam, BWR–LA, you're awesome for taking me on personally and knocking down doors! Jami Kandel, BWR–NY, here we go girl. To Susan Packard, my business consultant wonder woman! To my supportive L.A. girl squad: Leigh Collier, Carolyn Conrad, Kim McCoy, and Andrea Orbeck. To Alissa Pollack and Julie Talbott for believing in me and putting me on the airwaves. Thank you to Premiere Radio and my producers, David Bugenske and Susannah Eggleston. Jay Clarke and Magazines.com. Taylor Kahan at Crowd Surf. Stephanie and Wes Buttrey for my ever-changing and amazing website. The photographers: John Hall, Michael Gomez, Eric Anderson, Heather Anne Thomas, and Mark DeLong. Merri Lee at Gift & Gourmet. Rick and Robert at Bennett Galleries. Cielo Tabletop in Santa Fe. To Anderson Merchandisers and Bill Lardie for saying, "Of course we can!"

To my Nashville, Knoxville, Los Angeles, Scottsdale, and New York friends who continue to support my crazy schedule and dreams, which means I rarely get to see them! I love you all dearly.

Thank you,
Moll

DEDICATION

My mother is an extraordinary lady—strikingly beautiful, classy, sophisticated, emotional, strong, and passionate. It was difficult to choose just a few photos that truly capture her spirit, so these are my personal favorites. Her entire life, she immersed herself in whatever she believed would truly help or change others' lives. Whether it was her faith or the latest vitamin or product, it didn't matter; if she felt someone needed it, she was going to tell him why. My mother has an amazing photographic memory of scripture in the Bible, and

she can remember all the details from any movie set that she worked on—but don't ask her for directions!

Mary Ellen Kay (that's her stage name) was an actress under contract to Republic Studios. She has an impressive résumé, having starred in many movies, television episodes, and stage productions with big stars such as Roy Rogers, Buddy Ebsen, Lucille Ball, Mickey Rooney, and Anthony Quinn. She began her incredible career at age fifteen singing on the road with big bands. As a young starlet, Mom was even given the key to her city, Boardman, Ohio.

My mother has always been good at everything, including throwing a party at the drop of a hat, which she did all the time. I would often come home to a house full of people that I didn't even know. If mom found out that it was someone's birthday at church she would invite everyone over for brunch, and in no time flat serve a first-class buffet in the birthday person's honor. Every Thursday afternoon of my childhood, Mom hosted a Bible study. Women came from everywhere and filled our home to share and support each other. I grew up going to Scottsdale Christian Women's Club, revivals, Bible studies, and backstage at her television show called "The GAP" (God Answers Prayer). I marveled, even at a young age, that when a guest for the show couldn't make it, Mom would grab her microphone, sit in the chair, look straight into the camera—and it was a one-woman show. Now that I am in television and radio myself, I look back and realize what guts and fearless passion she truly had.

Today my mom, Mary Ellen Kay, is still a diva, amazingly gorgeous and a beautiful human being. Still a star with a full social calendar, now she's giving cocktail soirées, hosting Scrabble parties with her gal pals, and meeting for coffee with the one-legged bird (don't ask) and her dog, Belle.

Like most mothers and daughters, my mom and I have come full circle and we finally accept each other for all our quirks, talents, and most importantly, our human flaws. I love my mother very much and I dedicate this book to her. It is because of her that I live my life without fear, am inspired to help people, and love with everything that I have!

Thanks Mom, Mary Ellen "Kay" Ruffalo, for being you, otherwise I wouldn't be me! I love you always and forever.

Your daughter,
Molly
XO

TABLE OF CONTENTS

DECADENT
details

FROM THE COVER

9

FOREWORD

I read with great pleasure Moll Anderson's book, *The Seductive Home*, and enjoyed the world she so flawlessly created. I got lost in her ability to transform any space and make it uniquely her own, and came away with the feeling that I wanted to be able to do the same. I couldn't wait to see what she would come up with next!

Well, she did it, and it's wonderful!

Seductive Tables For Two

Tablescapes, Picnics, & Recipes That Inspire Romance

Her love and passion for what she does is evident on every page of her new book. You can feel and see the deep love and commitment she has for her family. Moll shares personal, insightful stories about herself and her family and explains why creating beautiful surroundings for large gatherings or for two is another way of showing love and appreciation.

Details, details, details! Moll's attention to the smallest of details is inspiring: the colors she chooses, the lighting, and the use of candles, music, flowers, and luscious fabrics! She explains why these elements are important and how to best utilize them to get the special effects you are looking for.

I really appreciated the tips Moll gives on the use of flowers, such as incorporating greenery from your garden to enhance the arrangement at no extra cost and choosing long-lasting blooms. Her tips are so practical, especially since the flowers I buy tend to only last a day and a half before I have to toss them! She also mentions the use of colored containers for effect and reveals how to keep the flowers standing tall.

Moll offers up little surprise ideas that will delight you and make you feel special. And isn't that what seduction is all about?

Her "Seductive Recipes for Two" section is right up my alley. Although Moll will occasionally phone it in, as she amply puts it, "It's fun to enjoy the sensuality of preparing a meal." She opens her chapter on Seductive Recipes for Two by starting with Praline To a Kiss French Toast. The afternoon and evening menus are carefully thought out, easy to prepare, and delicious. The Seduce Me Santa Fe chicken wrap is one of my favorites!

All the elements that you will need in order to create your own special seductive table for two are so beautifully photographed you can practically feel the fabric, smell the flowers, and taste the food. Every word and every detail are carefully thought out in order to give you the experience that Moll desires to share with you. She creates places of beauty, whether it's an outdoor picnic, an intimate cocktail in a small space, or a celebratory dinner in a dining room.

This lovely book is filled with passion for life and love of family, friends, and food. *Seductive Tables for Two* incorporates elegance, fantasy, sparkle, whimsy, glitz, glamour, and love. Oh dear, I just described Moll Anderson!

—Cristina Ferrare

Moll and Cristina
*Cristina Ferrare is an accomplished best-selling author,
television host, super model, wife and mother.*

THE MOST IMPORTANT TABLE YOU WILL EVER SET IS ONE THAT YOU WILL CREATE WITH YOUR ROMANTIC HEART

—MOLL

A seductive table for two is a tablescape set for ultimate romance, beckoning you with desire and fantasy. I call it "sensory tablescaping"; it seduces all of your senses: taste, touch, sight, scent, and sound.

Why do you need a table for two? So many of life's special moments are celebrated around the table. It's about being face to face, looking into each other's eyes, and really seeing your loved one. It's important that you and your partner set aside time to share a meal together, a cup of coffee and croissant, or a glass of wine coupled with cheese and crackers. It's not about clearing your schedule completely and slaving for hours in the kitchen or spending a fortune to create an atmosphere. It's about stopping and remembering what's truly important—each other—because you are the foundation of your family.

I am excited to share my secrets with you about having a sexy, fun, and exciting relationship, and it all starts by simply creating memorable meals with your partner. It is key, however, that you find a true partner in life—someone who is partnership oriented. Why be in a relationship with someone who is not wholly committed to the partnership? This is a question I should have asked myself more often. Such a simple, seemingly obvious question, and yet few really consider it or understand the significance of becoming a couple when searching for Mr. or Mrs. Right. There's a great quote I adore: *"What is love, if it's not to make life easier for the one that we love."* I think that when two people are absolutely the right match for one another, they want the very best for each other, to live in joy and gratefulness, even through the toughest of times.

Several years ago Charlie and I went through one of the most incredibly difficult years of our lives. My husband was forced to close his family business, which was devastating and unbelievably stressful—and which occurred the exact same time his oldest son, Chase, collapsed from a blood clot that went straight to his brain. We spent months in shock, going between the hospitals and rehabilitation. I cannot begin to express the level of fear that goes through you when your child is hurting or facing death. I know some of you can empathize only too well. What got Charlie and me through this time, besides our faith, was the fact that even if it was just for an hour in those twenty-four hours of stress, we would go back to our hotel room, order a glass of wine, and talk about how lucky we were. Some days we had to work at it, but we always found something for which to be thankful each day. We always knew that we had each other for support. Going through an experience such as ours, we realized just how blessed we are and were amazed at the strength we gained in return.

I believe everything happens exactly the way it's supposed to! Chase is a walking miracle, at 100 percent today and doing great. We are a fortunate family.

People are always asking me how Charlie and I manage to function while maintaining such crazy schedules. We spend hundreds of hours a year on a plane traveling for business and are in constant packing and unpacking mode. Truth be told, we complement each other. We both love to travel and find it exciting, and we both love to get home and snuggle in; our home is truly our sanctuary. I love the saying, "Home is where the heart is"; so for me, wherever my husband is, whether in the air, in another city, at the office, or at home, that is where my heart is! Connecting daily still holds true for us. I encourage you to show that you care—express interest in your partner's day, career, and dreams. That's what a partnership is about.

My desire is that you'll use this book and your surroundings as a guide to creating the perfect *table pour deux*. Whether elegant, casual, impromptu, or on-the-go, whether a beautifully decorated table, sexy tray of treats, or even a romantic picnic—it can be the making of an intimate connection. All you need to do is make it happen!

It truly doesn't matter whether you are newlyweds, empty nesters, in a committed relationship, or parents who no longer find the time to spend alone together—you need to find a way back to the two of you. One simple and easy way to do that is to begin with a seductive table for two. You may think you're just too busy and can't find a spare moment. If that's the case, then I'm telling you right now that you can't afford not to create a table for two!

You need to treat this experience as a date. Plan for a simple weekly rendezvous and light up the romance with sensory tablescaping. And you won't even have to leave the house.

In *Seductive Tables for Two,*™ I share with you my table for two inspirations, from romantic to whimsical presentations, holiday and anytime celebrations. Inside the book, I reveal my must-haves to creating a sensory-scaped table, with plenty of helpful hints, how-

to's, and all the essentials to add the decadent details to any dining experience. You'll find simple recipes, fun and delicious cocktails for two, and creative ways of dressing up take-out from your favorite restaurants. With just the right information and a wealth of inspiration, you will be on your way to creating your own uniquely seductive tables and most importantly, discovering true passion.

WHAT ARE YOU WAITING FOR?
—MOLL

ELEGANCE

ROMANCE

PASSION

SEDUCTIVE
TABLES FOR TWO

Getting to express myself to you about the importance of intimate dining and creating elegant, fun, and whimsical memories is truly like Christmas for me. I believe that in this lifetime – that's today, right this minute – you absolutely need to seize the moment and get in touch with your dreams and desires for your relationship. Do you even remember what they were? Or better yet, what they should or can be? Is happiness on that list? Are you happy? Are you loving your spouse or partner like there's no tomorrow? Do you feel the love? I am here to give you written permission to feel – LIVE! Live your dreams in the midst of all the "real world" challenges thrown at you: children, carpools, work and overextending yourself. I believe 100 percent in my heart in the art of dining for two – Seductive tables for two, to be exact! Will dining for two solve world crises? No, but Seductive Tables for Two will encourage you to start taking the time to dream and experience romance again and, in turn, realize that it's as easy as saying, "I'm going to do it today!"

Mell

I hope this chapter gives you lots of ideas, maybe even inspires you to do something out of your comfort zone—anything! I want you to pay attention to just how easy and simple it is to create a seductive table for two. My five must-haves are back, and these are key to making your life and the experience simple: color, lighting, music, flowers, and fabric. These essential elements all possess important but different characteristics to bring your table together.

COLOR—A marvelous form of energy, color has an amazing impact on the human psyche. Did you know that each color has an energy specific to it? Consider hues for your tablescapes that naturally draw your attention and evoke the sensual response you are searching for.

LIGHTING—A flip of the switch or the strike of a match changes the mood of every setting. But more than that, mood lighting is a natural phenomenon. An overcast day, a romantic sunset, or a brilliant, mysterious full moon—lighting affects us on a primal level. We are innately programmed to be moved by light, so use this easy tool to create the perfect atmosphere for your table for two.

MUSIC—Set the atmosphere thermostat to fit the mood you desire in any space you want. In many ways, music is the most versatile lifestyle accessory. So decorate your table with sound. Not only can music ripple through a room with incredible power but it can also bring a new spark to your relationship.

FLOWERS—These extraordinarily versatile table accessories come in a variety of colors, sizes, and scents, perfect for a wide range of settings. It's been proven that women automatically feel more romantic when in the presence of these wonderful blooms.

FABRIC—One of the most telling elements in a space is fabric. It adds texture and a wealth of personality. Linens can add that bit of pizzazz to spice up your table; from the color to texture to the details, there are so many choices! One of the few design elements geared to the sense of touch, fabric welcomes you with comfort.

COLOR

COLOR IS A MARVELOUS FORM OF ENERGY.

LIGHTING

WE ARE MOVED BY LIGHT, SO USE THIS EASY TOOL
TO CREATE THE PERFECT SENSUAL ATMOSPHERE.

MUSIC

MUSIC IS THE MOST VERSATILE LIFESTYLE ACCESSORY,
SO DECORATE YOUR TABLE WITH SOUND.

FLOWERS

IT'S BEEN PROVEN THAT WOMEN AUTOMATICALLY FEEL MORE
ROMANTIC WHEN IN THE PRESENCE OF BLOOMS.

FABRIC

LINENS CAN ADD THAT BIT OF PIZZAZZ TO SPICE UP YOUR
TABLE, FROM THE COLOR TO TEXTURE AND DETAILS.
THERE ARE SO MANY CHOICES!

Luscious
IN LAVENDER

LUSCIOUS IN LAVENDER

This table makes my heart sing every time I look at it! It's totally intoxicating to me and appeals to the senses. Savor the hue of the sterling roses. Adding flowers to the table not only adds color to your tablescape but they add a delicate scent as well. I was inspired by the soft lavender color of the roses and let my imagination take over to create this luscious sensory-scaped table. I know some of you are probably saying right now that you're not capable of "sensory tablescaping." Well, you just might surprise yourself and your partner.

Build your table by adding my must-haves of tablescaping: color, lighting, music, flowers, and fabric—but start simple first. Choose the fabric and textures, and then layer with your accessories to add the color, scent, and lighting. The details will begin to emerge as you add the elements to your table, and your simple yet stunning table will begin to reflect your sense of what is beautiful, special, and perfect for you.

I love the Walt Disney quote that says, "You can dream, create, design and build the most wonderful place in the world, but it requires people to make the dream reality." I believe that the same holds true for the perfect seductive table for two. You can set the most incredible ambiance with the perfect lighting, the most spectacular flowers, the most fabulous wine and delectable food, but it requires two hearts to join in the magic.

DECADENT *details*

Whether the celebration is inside or outside, call on the decadent details to guide your inspiration. The details will help you quickly gather all the essentials needed to create the ultimate little dinner party for two. For this table, the details came to life—everything from the color of my linens to the choice of my dishes to the lavender roses. Once you start seeing your space in decadent details you will be surprised how each time you get started, your brain will begin thinking in the *details*. Create a decadent details guide as a tool to simplify your life and home so that you will have a handy resource. Think of your detail guide as an inventory of your table wardrobe, home, accessories, and special treasures. It can be organized digitally so you can carry it with you on your mobile device or you can print it to make your own book. A book or file of your decadent details not only becomes a handy reference to completing a table for two in an unexpected room; it also becomes your own private workbook of your space. An organized book will be helpful in any future decorating plans for home, events, or updating your accessories.

Fun Fact: Lavender roses have been said to symbolize love at first sight and enchantment.

SURPRISE ME!

What makes this table special are the little surprises hidden away. Imagine
sitting at the table, sipping your champagne and enjoying your meal, when
suddenly your eyes catch a special something tucked within. It might be
something you have been dreaming about, or it may be a treasured memento
from a once shared experience, or even a trinket that reminds them of you. It
doesn't have to be expensive. The thoughtfulness of the gift will surely add an
individual touch to an already wonderful evening. Think about something small
they may have mentioned long ago. If your partner hasn't mentioned a special
something they desire, I suggest dreaming in color. If their favorite color is
blue, choose a gift that goes with the color scheme. If it is a special event or an
anniversary, you may want that moment to be the inspiration for your surprise
and your table for two.

FLOWERS

One of my must-haves, flowers, evoke sensory responses through both sight and smell.

- Use flowers and greenery found in your yard as a natural and beautiful way to incorporate flowers at no extra cost.

- Grabbing a bouquet while at the market will make life one-less-stop easier. If you want a long-lasting flower, choose alstroemeria, which lasts up to a month and comes in many colors.

- Consider using a colored container as a fun way to add a special decadent detail.

- Orchid sprays, roses, gladiolas, daylilies, cosmos, and snapdragons are just a few selections that will work beautifully in a tall bud vase.

- Bunch small florals together in a container for more visual appeal.

- Secure your flowers in place by creating a grid with waterproof tape. This will keep your flowers standing tall and will help with flower grouping.

- Remove leaves below the waterline in your vase and add a few drops of bleach or vodka to the water before arranging.

FIND A
BEAUTIFUL
PLACE
AND GET LOST

—UNKNOWN

Sensual
SEA ESCAPE

SENSUAL SEA ESCAPE

A sunset-toned private little shrimp cocktail for two is a perfect way to begin a seductive Sunday afternoon. Of course, as always, you can prepare just about anything to serve for your lunch, but these are simple and easy ideas to get you started. Then it's up to you. There's no end to the possibilities of what you may want to serve and to create for your intimate setting.

   To create this sensual escape, I began by dressing the table full of romance. Fabric is one of my design must-haves; it adds color and texture and sets the vibe for the style in the room. A tablecloth is not only the first step in how to set a table properly but it is also a key sensory element because it appeals to the sense of touch. A simple, classic linen tablecloth is a great staple to have on hand for setting an elegant table for two, but it's also fun to add a variety of fabrics to your tables. Layering linens is one way to build texture and change the style of your tablescape. For a romantic style, add a lace overlay; for a touch of whimsy or a casual theme, add a patterned or colorful table runner or layer with placemats. Don't be afraid to think outside traditional table linens. Dress up your table using what you already have. A favorite scarf or shawl will add a personal touch to your table. If you have a beautiful tabletop you want to showcase, you don't have to use a tablecloth—you can add texture through decorative placemats and cloth napkins. Cloth napkins are an essential accessory to creating a sensory-scaped table and a simple way to enhance the look and style of your table setting.

DECADENT *details*

When I pulled out my decadent details guide to be inspired I couldn't help but bask in the tones of this room. They are so scrumptious! Choosing colors that blend beautifully together is the ultimate in creating a soothing room with a balanced feel. For this special afternoon, the details complemented the regal gilded gold accents in this room; the crystal goblets, the bowls, and the china all became the perfect choice for a gorgeous table setting that enhanced the details of the room. The linens were two antique cloths I picked up in Santa Fe, and a remnant piece of fabric that I simply knotted at the corners as a quick fix.

I let the jewel-encrusted napkin rings inspire my decision to serve seafood at this brunch. The decision of shrimp cocktail with a fabulous red sauce was easy! It was either that or a night of desserts, maybe bowls full of mounding scoops of mango, peach, and blood-orange sorbet! When more than one great idea comes to you, remember to save it for next time. Jot it down in your guide and also save a date for it. You'll be a pro before you know it.

CENTER OF ATTENTION

Every table needs a focal point.

- Have a collection of glass vases on hand for your floral centerpieces, but choose one in the right proportion to your arrangement. The general rule is to place your flowers about $1^1/_2$ times the height of your vase or container and be careful to balance the width with the height.

- Think outside the vase. Pitchers are a popular choice for flower arrangements. Choose a size and color that complements your flower choices. Consider plants in colorful pots or tin pails.

- A general rule is to keep your centerpiece low so you can see your partner across the table. Branches can create a simple but beautiful centerpiece, but make sure these do not obstruct your view. You can fill your vessel with a variety of fruits, vegetables, pebbles, shells, holiday décor, and more to add color and interest.

- A selection of candles in a variety of sizes will illuminate your table. Choose a variety of heights and an uneven number for your grouping; three or five work best. Glass and metal lanterns are also ideal for your candle presentation.

- Look for unexpected treasures to anchor the center of your table—lamps, statues, picture frames, or even a beautiful tray.

Fun Fact: The popular term *china* used for fine plates and bowls was coined by the Europeans. The highly valued bowls, plates, and other decorative wares were imported from China over a span of hundreds of years. The Chinese developed the technique more than a thousand years ago and were its sole makers until the 18th century. We can give a big thanks to the Chinese for giving us a kick start to all the fabulous china we now use to create our tables for two.

TABLE LINENS

You never know where you will find a future seductive table topper or cloth that's truly a treasure, so always be on the lookout!

- Antique stores and flea markets are great places to find gorgeous old tapestries and tablecloths that may only look worn. Once washed and pressed, they can be a great find.

- Keep your eyes open for expensive fabrics that have been cut and placed in the remnant section of your neighborhood fabric store.

- Use scarves you love and wear for table toppers. You already chose them because you were drawn to them for their beautiful and colorful fabric. Remember C.P.U.: cost per use.

- Believe it or not, antique blankets, throws, and bedspreads can make great-looking tablecloths.

- If you are feeling very creative and have some extra time, visit your local art store to pick up a lightweight canvas drop cloth and paint it the perfect color for your setting.

Always remember, there are no rules! Think outside the box.

WHAT I LOVE MOST ABOUT MY HOME IS WHO I SHARE IT WITH

—MOLL

ARTICHOKE *Affair*

ARTICHOKE AFFAIR

A sensual tablescape can be conjured at any moment. As for my artichoke affair—it was inspired in my little Santa Fe guesthouse while I was busy preparing the space for a visit from friends. As I was arranging all the fresh flowers on the bedside tables, I decided to take a moment and indulge in a cup of hot coffee. I began to look around and marvel at the courtyard views on either side of the room. How had this view been missed before? It only takes a minute to gain a fresh perspective in an old place. Talk about atmosphere! Wow! With both sets of the double doors open it was as if I had been transported to a far-away land, suddenly in a quaint countryside garden and yet completely indoors. I sat there content in the joy of my moment and thought, "What a stunning place to share a table for two." This room is normally arranged with four reading chairs that face each other joined by a small table just large enough for a tray. In the morning, it's perfect for guests to wake up with a cup of coffee and read the paper, but I had certainly not thought of creating a seductive table for two here—yet!

So, it all starts with just a drop of a fresh new vision. That's how the idea begins to happen. Nothing is impossible; you just need to let go and begin to live a seductive lifestyle and you will stop concentrating on the cannots of the day and start creating the ideas you have in your imagination. With a perfect table for two—that folds up neatly and can easily be carried from room to room or place to place—you, too, can create anything, anywhere, anytime. Most importantly, it won't break the bank to do this.

48

DECADENT *details*

Santa Fe afternoons are spectacular in the summer because the altitude is approximately 7,000 feet. It may be 90 degrees outside during the day, but in the shade it's magically cool and makes for a lovely tête-à-tête. The decadent details of the linens were a passionate plum hue with embroidered artichokes. Honestly, these were chosen for the color alone and then when I pulled them out to start designing my tabletop, I found myself amazed at the beautiful artichoke design incorporated into the linens. It hit me so instantly—why not play off this theme for my menu?

For some silly traditional reason, I had only ever served my artichokes for dinner, not any other time of the day, so the afternoon would be a fun switch from our normal routine! When you allow all the elements to tell the story, you allow the ultimate table for two to arrive. Yes, I could have served just about anything, but this time I was being led by the details. A picture speaks a thousand words.

ARRANGING WITH EDIBLES

As you know, flowers are one of my important must-haves for sensory tablescaping. But there are many things you can add to your floral arrangement to enhance the beauty and interest of your display.

One of the most popular additions is seasonal edibles.

- Imagine the beauty of cranberries floating in a vase filled with fabulous florals as a Thanksgiving centerpiece.

- Don't forget about pumpkins and squashes to bring the harvest season to life.

- Pomegranates, oranges, berries, and even cinnamon sticks can be added to wreaths and centerpieces, bringing a scent of the holiday season to the table.

- Think beyond the traditional holiday celebrations and add fresh seasonal edibles to complete your table theme. Bright red peppers bring a splash of color to a fiesta, and farmers' market finds of carrots and radishes add a dash of fun to a spring or Easter celebration.

- For this table I found some beautiful miniature (baby) artichokes and deep aubergine eggplants to add to my Artichoke Affair. Not only does it carry out my artichoke theme, it adds the perfect color and texture to my relaxed and earthy setting.

Fun Fact: Ancient Greeks and Romans considered artichokes to be aphrodisiacs, and in the 16th century, only men were allowed to eat them. Women were prohibited from eating artichokes in many countries because they were still considered to have aphrodisiac properties and were thought to enhance sexual power.

TABLE FOR TWO

- Antique wine tables make fabulous tables for two. They are most commonly made out of wood and have the ability to fold up flat. They are ideal for storing away when not in use.

- Never underestimate a good old-fashioned card table. They get the job done. Just be sure to have linens on hand. They hide a multitude of not-so-aesthetically pleasing vinyl and metal.

- Coffee tables are a great option anytime you simply don't have a table or you desire a bohemian vibe. Just make sure to add large pillows to sit on.

- You could actually use a large end table. Make sure the table legs are strategically placed in a way that is comfortable to sit at for both of you.

- Bistro tables come in many varieties: from indoor, outdoor, metal, wood, glass-top, metal-top, and at any price point as well.

- Look for inexpensive table rounds that are easy to transport and store. Common sizes for two are 24", 28", and 30" in diameter.

IT'S NOT ABOUT THE SIZE OF THE TABLE; IT'S WHAT YOU PUT ON IT

—MOLL

Fresh & Flirty
PASTA

FRESH AND FLIRTY PASTA

Sometimes a request is made for something familiar and comforting, like an old favorite family meal. In my house we have several. When my husband asked about the pasta with olive oil, fresh peppers, and Parmesan cheese, I immediately realized that this pasta needed a much sexier name, especially if it was one of his favorites! So I started the plan by appropriately naming it "Fresh and Flirty Pasta!"

Remember, you can give great meaning to very simple things, even pasta. This pasta is really easy, so just a quick stop at my favorite grocery store to pick up the ingredients for the pasta, a salad, and flowers was all I needed to do. Music is never an issue because I have a seductive playlist for just about any possible celebration with my husband. The most important and only thing left was to decide where to set up my table for two to serve this Fresh and Flirty Pasta. Why? Because, why not? It was Friday and we had nowhere to be the next day, so date night it was. Take the lead and let your spouse or partner know that you took the time to make the evening just a little bit more special than usual. It's important to change the location of where you dine or have a cocktail because you will immediately break the monotonous behavior that has become routine. Sometimes that's all you need to spark a bit of excitement. As you can see, this is a very simple location and table setting. Nothing over the top or super glamorous, just simple and very unexpected to my husband—and really, that's all that matters.

DECADENT *details*

The strongest detail in this setting is the table. It's actually a wine tasting table that houses bottles of wine below. This is one of my favorite tables because its industrial nature lends itself to a hip, masculine vibe. I think that anytime you pick a strong, manly setting it immediately puts your spouse or partner at ease. Toss in a pop of color with flowers, and that is all the softness you need. Women and men alike will love this casual atmosphere because it's totally down to earth. The details here all work well with one another— wood, metal, wire, animal print, and neutral tones. From the silverware to the napkin rings, the antler candlesticks and hand-shaped pottery; it all goes together without feeling too matchy. This table setting is one that works incredibly well in many different environments. No thinking is required when pulling this tablescape together, simply grab the glasses or linens that you love and then make magic!

THE FRESH FACTOR

SPRING:

Apricots
Artichokes
Asparagus
Grapefruit
Green onions
Leeks
Lemons
Lettuce
Mushrooms
Parsley
Radishes
Rhubarb
Spinach
Spring onions
Strawberries
Wild greens

SUMMER:

Apples
Avocado
Basil
Bell pepper
Berries
Carrots
Cherries
Cilantro
Cucumbers
Eggplant
Garlic
Green beans
Mangoes
Melon

Nectarines
Okra
Peaches
Peppers
Summer squash
Tomatoes
Zucchini

AUTUMN:

Arugula
Broccoli
Brussels sprouts
Cauliflower

Collards
Chiles
Cranberries
Fennel
Grapes
Kale
Lemongrass
Limes
Pomegranates
Pumpkin
Shallots
Swiss chard
Winter squash

WINTER:

Beets
Belgian endive
Cabbage
Celery
Citrus
Clementines
Escarole
Horseradish
Kiwi
Mandarins
Parsnips
Pears

Rutabagas
Sweet potatoes
Turnips

YEAR-ROUND:

Apples
Carrots
Herbs
Onions
Potatoes

Fun Fact: Stoneware is a man-made stone that is shaped into dishes and fired at very high temperatures. The firing melts all tiny holes, keeping it non-porous, impervious to liquids, very scratch resistant, and oven safe. Earthenware is formed by a mixture made of clay and is fired at a lower temperature, resulting in a porous surface that absorbs liquids and is prone to scratches. This low-fired clay cannot withstand high temperatures, so it is not safe for oven use.

CANDLES

Candles are one of my most essential must-haves when creating a seductive home, seductive table for two, or sensual celebration! There's nothing like the flicker of candlelight!

- Your home should have a signature scent just like you. However, when placing candles on a table, make sure the candles are completely unscented so they don't compete with the sumptuous food.

- Candles should be trimmed to ¼ inch before you light them. A properly trimmed wick will burn longer and reduce smoke and soot.

- For the ambiance, even if you do not intend to burn the candles, the wick on each candle should be briefly lit to give it a charred look. It will also make lighting later quick and easy.

- Candles in votives placed in large amounts all over the room is a fabulous and inexpensive way to create drama and "wow" for very little expense.

DINNER FOR TWO, CANDLELIGHT, AND MUSIC INVITE YOUR ROMANTIC IMAGINATION TO GO WILD

—MOLL

Savory
SUNRISE

SAVORY SUNRISE

Nothing says romance like the color of red bursting from the beautiful bloom of a rose! I was so in love with these particular roses that I picked up from a local flower stand, I thought, why not serve one on a plate as if it were part of my breakfast for two? Remember that everything you create should speak to your senses. When a red rose is rested on your plate along with fresh baked pastries, you simply can't help but pick up that rose the second you sit down at this brilliant red table setting. The fragrant smell of the flower is an intoxicating sensual awakening. Don't underestimate the power of the flower; it captures the senses in a most unique way and the senses play a tremendous part in capturing one's heart. Everything on these plates is just one easy stop at your favorite little corner bakery or store. The most wonderful thing about this breakfast is that the small amount of time you spend setting up this scenario will bring a valuable return in your romantic relationship. Add a little living color into your life. The color red is a very intense hue, so grab those ruby roses while at the grocery, or think a red-hot nightie, fabulous red lips, or luxurious crimson sheets. If you add red to your space, you'll immediately awaken your morning and life.

DECADENT *details*

Featured in this table is a set of fabulous red Hermès china. But don't let the price tag of this exquisite china scare you—instead, allow it to inspire you! I use everything in my tables to show you that it doesn't have to cost a fortune and it doesn't matter where your details come from. What matters is when they come together on a table for two they are actually becoming your own decadent details. The more expensive china is wonderful, but the truth is that this setting could have been replaced with simple white dishes and still looked phenomenal. The red linens layered underneath the napkins are actually dishtowels, but they add a most exciting pop of color. The table itself is metal with the look of wrought iron, which I picked up from a yard sale. My favorite part of this tabletop is the beautiful old Spanish lace piece that I found in Santa Fe at a precious little shop. This table has a feeling that is collected, special, and deliciously decadent.

JOY OF COLOR

The colors you choose for your seductive tablescape will set the vibe for your dining experience.

- A quiet intimate or elegant table will call for a more subtle color palette such as lavender, pale blue, or creamy yellow.

- To bring out your vibrant or wild side, choose hot, bright colors such as hot pink, bright yellow, and vibrant orange.

- Want a beachy getaway? Set the tone with soft blues and creamy whites.

- Warm, spice-inspired hues of chili powder, red pepper, paprika, and cayenne are sure to add some heat to your table. These earthy tones are perfect complements to a harvest meal.

- The ultimate color of romance is red, so be sure and have a go-to selection of red tableware linens to set the sexy tone for your dining experience.

Fun Fact: A full rose typically has around 40 petals on each head. The higher number of petals, the more luscious the flower.

BREAKFAST TRAY CHECKLIST

Having a tray on hand for a seductive meal for two is essential. Trays are handy additions to your table wardrobe and are perfect not just for breakfast in bed but also for cocktails, appetizers, and dessert get-togethers.

- Fresh fruit—strawberries, blueberries, grapes, oranges, apples, bananas
- Toast (frozen bread tastes fresh after popping it in the toaster)
- Croissants, bagels, English muffins
- Jam, butter, honey
- Cereal
- Pancake mix or French toast & syrup
- Eggs
- Juice, milk, coffee, or tea
- Flowers: can be a single stem or a small, compact arrangement. Keep it low and small so it fits on the tray.
- Candle votives
- Silverware and napkins
- Plates, bowls, mugs or cups, and saucers
- Small coffee pot (single cup brewers are quick and easy options)
- Cream and sugar
- Salt and pepper shakers

ROMANCE
IS THE GLAMOUR
WHICH TURNS THE DUST
OF EVERYDAY LIFE
INTO A GOLDEN HAZE

—AMANDA CROSS

DESTINATION

IMPROMPTU

FANTASY

SEDUCTION
TO GO

Stop and toss out all your old thinking when it comes to how mealtime is supposed to be. Shake off some of the old rules of what it means to be a great wife that you've been hearing from your mom and your mom's mother and all those folks that wouldn't be caught dead ordering a pizza or picking up food to go. I respect all those amazing women and men that slave over the stove and manage to do it all. I honestly love to do that MOST of the time, but at other times, I'm just happy to give myself permission to do whatever it takes to put something on the table or tray or even a blanket for a picnic. Sometimes that means takeout, delivery, or something quick and easy that I can throw together in order to simply do what's truly important - spend quality time with my husband! I'm not trying to discourage you from learning to cook I'm trying to encourage you to pick and choose how much time you spend in the kitchen so you can find more time for romance.
What are you waiting for?

Mel

Who doesn't love getting away from it all? Even if it's just in your imagination. There's nothing like a change of scenery or a night off from cooking to free up your romantic mind. Seduction To Go is packed full of fun and easy ideas to help you escape the norm and get back into the mood for a little relationship building. My must-haves are theme, location, preparation, fantasy, and of course, the sips & bits—no picnic-to-go would be complete without a bite to eat.

THEME—If you dream it, you can create it—all you need is a vision. Transport yourself to any destination; from the fiesta flavors of Mexico to the rich, seductive atmosphere of France, you can bring your favorite travel memories to your table theme. Or you can create your seductive soirée-to-go from an exciting scene you saw in a movie that spoke to your heart.

LOCATION—Location, location, location—it's everything. Where you choose to have your table or picnic for two will set the tone for your meal. Even the simplest space at night will be a stunning location with just votives and music. Set in a private place in the woods, or under a canopy overlooking the water, it is sure to be memorable. The scenes for romance are everywhere; you just need to know how and where to find them.

PREPARATION—When you live a full life, it's important to prioritize your relationship and spend special quality time together. So take a little bit of time to plan in advance. Keep your pantry and bar stocked with the essential sips and bits. Have your picnic basket and groundcover ready, and with your decadent details guide you will know what you have on hand to sensory-scape any gathering for two.

FANTASY—This is where I tell you to completely let go and have a blast! There is no right or wrong here. Fantasy is personal! A great relationship requires shutting out the rest of the world every once in awhile. Get lost in your imagination; a magical, sensually creative night is also an unforgettable night.

SIPS & BITS—Take it out or take it in. Take a drive through the country, pull over, spread a blanket, and have a little snack with a few sips of wine. Fast and fabulous eats take you out of the kitchen and into a fun-filled date with your partner. It doesn't matter what you eat; it matters that you take the time to do it.

THEME

IF YOU DREAM IT, YOU CAN CREATE IT... ALL YOU NEED IS A VISION.

LOCATION

THE SCENES FOR ROMANCE ARE EVERYWHERE; YOU JUST NEED TO KNOW HOW AND WHERE TO FIND THEM.

PREPARATION

WHEN YOU LIVE A FULL LIFE, IT'S IMPORTANT TO PRIORITIZE YOUR RELATIONSHIP AND SPEND QUALITY TIME TOGETHER. SO TAKE A LITTLE BIT OF TIME TO PLAN IN ADVANCE.

FANTASY

GET LOST IN THE INVITATION OF YOUR IMAGINATION; A MAGICAL, SENSUALLY CREATIVE NIGHT IS ALSO AN UNFORGETTABLE NIGHT.

SIPS & BITS

FAST AND FABULOUS EATS TAKE YOU OUT OF THE KITCHEN AND INTO A FUN-FILLED DATE WITH YOUR PARTNER.

Passionate
PICNIC

PASSIONATE PICNIC

There's nothing like a passionate setting for a seductive picnic! It's all about the atmosphere and location, location, location! When you have time to plan, then by all means, the sky is the limit. If you are going for impromptu, then the floor in your master bedroom will work perfectly to set down a blanket and set up a meal. This particular celebration was my chance to call on a fantasy I had long forgotten about. I love the movie *Robin Hood*. Everything about it is so intensely romantic, and the feasts are fabulously grand right in the middle of the woods. The idea about recreating my own version of "What would Maid Marian do?" was definitely calling to me.

So one day I thought, why not? I grabbed my new colorful blanket and all the sexy pillows I could carry and created my own forest in my backyard.

I inlcuded all the essentials of sensory tablescaping: plates, silverware, tablecloth and napkins, candelabra, flowers, and music. This was not a paper plate and plastic utensil event. I was seducing my partner, not planning a tailgate. I added some wine, fruit and cheese, and other assorted goodies that seemed appropriate. The last ingredient, of course, was a fabulous dress.

DECADENT *details*

A nice level patch of grass and some beautiful trees for shade are all you need to pull together a perfect passionate picnic. Why not create your very own sensual soirée wherever you are: at your home, your yard, or a destination picnic location? Using my five must-haves in the details, I pulled together the fabric with a colorful blanket and then used an eclectic grouping of pillows. I added the fabulous florals, which paved the way for a colorful, romantic, and sexy picnic full of frolicking. Some wine, cheese and crackers, and other tasty appetizers were beautifully placed in the picnic basket and throughout the comfortable spread. The iron platters and leather tray contrasted with the cut glass and overflowing fruit, forming the perfect balance of strong masculine and feminine touches. This scenario truly speaks to all of your senses and brings the fantasy to life.

TYPES OF CHEESE

Fresh: These unripened cheeses, such as cream cheese, cottage cheese, and ricotta, are very soft and mild and are commonly used in baking.

Stretch-Curd: These cheeses melt smoothly and are also good for slicing and using in sandwiches. Mozzarella is a popular mild and creamy cheese.

Soft-Ripened: Brie, Boursault, and Camembert, for example, are uncooked, unpressed, and only aged for a short time, producing a soft, spreadable texture.

Semi-Soft: Including Havarti, Monterey Jack, and Muenster varieties, these are cooked but not pressed, making them perfect to slice for bread or crackers, or for melting on baked dishes and sandwiches.

Semifirm: Asiago, Cheddar, Edam, Fontina, Gouda, Gruyere, and Swiss are examples of uncooked, pressed, and aged cheese. These cheeses have a density that is ideal for eating with crackers, bread, fruit, and sandwiches.

Firm (Hard): Cooked, pressed, and aged, the compact texture of Parmesan and Pecorino Romano make them perfect for grating to garnish on top of dishes.

Blue-Veined: Gorgonzola, Maytag Blue, and Roquefort have a strong flavor and typically can be crumbled, spread, or sliced, depending on moisture content.

Goat's Milk: Goat's milk cheeses are generally milky and creamy and sometimes slightly tangy.

PACKING YOUR PICNIC

BASKET: There are numerous options for packing your picnic essentials, from the traditional picnic baskets to canvas totes with handles to wire baskets. Choose one that is strong enough to hold your plates and heavier essentials. Layer your heavier items first and use your linens to protect your breakables.

WHAT TO PACK?

SOFT GOODS: Tablecloth and napkins; large blanket, quilt, or mat; pillows

HARD GOODS: Dinnerware; glassware; silverware; cooler; vase or basket for flowers; seductive spices (Tabasco, ketchup, mustard, salt & pepper— whatever your heart desires)

AMBIANCE: Candles; flowers; music: iPod, portable speakers, or radio (check batteries beforehand); lanterns

OTHER PICNIC ESSENTIALS: Corkscrew or bottle opener; lighter for the candles; hand cleaner or wipes; trash bags for clean-up afterward

FOOD AND DRINK: This can be as simple or as complicated as you have time for. You can cook, order to-go, or just use items on hand in your pantry and fridge.

SHARING A PICNIC IS A CELEBRATION OF THE ONE YOU'RE WITH

—UNKNOWN

Hot
DIGGITY DOG

Fun Fact: The term *hot dog* was brought to life during a Giants game when sports cartoonist Tad Dorgan published an image of dachshund dogs barking. He penned "hot dog" because he didn't know how to spell *dachshund*, so he abbreviated to *dog*. The term first appeared in the Oxford English Dictionary in 1900.

HOT DIGGITY DOG

I want you to not only *see* fireworks this Fourth of July, I want you to experience real fireworks, the kind that go off in your heart and head when you kiss under the stars or embrace with passion. I want you to connect to how it all began between the two of you. Turn up the heat with your sweetheart through a simple but fabulous hot dog picnic for two. Grab all your favorite hot and spicy toppings to create the ultimate gourmet hot dog experience. This is one of those meals where it's definitely not about extravagance. When you are well prepared, all your happenings are low maintenance, super easy, and fun. This little cookout in your backyard, park, or on your apartment balcony will leave you seeing sparks everywhere.

DECADENT *details*

Pump up an ordinary barbecue with some pizazz and sparkle! The thing I love about serving good ole American hot dogs is that you can dress them up or dress them down. That goes for your picnic table or trays as well. This is where really knowing your partner's favorite condiments and specialty foods helps in making your choices for the perfect Hot Diggity Dog. Grab all his or her favorite chips, pickles, sauces, beer, and salads—the works! Throw them all in for an exciting overload of flavors and delicacies. There is nothing like a buffet of all the things you love with the one you love. The design elements add the tone, whether it's fun gingham plates with painted ants scurrying around or trays you can carry from the kitchen to your backyard.

Since this is a Fourth of July night, the key element, of course, is TNT Sparklers to set off the night with some sizzle. Think about adding them into your table setting, or maybe have your dessert arrive with them lighting up the path as you make a stellar entrance. All of this is just simply meant to be great fun with a seductive twist that will make your Fourth of July one you'll be fantasizing about for a long time.

COOKOUT CHECKLIST

When planning a cookout for two, it is helpful to have a handy checklist:

- **Main Meal:** Your main course will determine the rest of your menu. For a simple cookout, choose hot dogs, hamburgers, or chicken. You can also try a twist on the grilled hamburger by offering a turkey, tuna, or veggie burger.

- **Side dishes:** Include the classic cookout sides of baked beans, macaroni and cheese, cole slaw, pasta and potato salads, corn on the cob, and chips. These are all items you can pick up at any deli or supermarket. Don't be afraid to add your own unique touch to the classic favorites.

- **Condiments:** Your selection of condiments can make a big difference in turning an ordinary cookout into something wonderful. In addition to the must-haves of ketchup, mustard, mayo, barbecue sauce, and relish, add your favorites to the menu and don't be afraid to spice it up. Ramp up your toppings with jalapeños, pickles, sauerkraut, coleslaw, lettuce, and freshly grown tomatoes. Create your own special sauces and relishes by combining your favorite staples. See page 209 to learn how to embellish with relish.

- **Dessert:** Nothing says summer like the taste of fresh berries, melons, peaches, and plums. Berries and peaches over ice cream is an easy and delicious option if your cookout is close to a freezer, or try a store-bought pound cake and add fruit—and don't forget the whipped cream.

ALFRESCO ENTERTAINING

When the weather heats up, it's time to move the party outdoors! Whether you're taking advantage of a sunny afternoon or a cooler evening, you can make the most of a summer soirée for two by incorporating these simple—but important—details that add pizzazz to any casual get-together.

- Forget the paper and plastic and use real silverware and napkins to add an elegant touch to your tablescapes.

- If you must, opt for non-breakable dishes such as melamine to avoid any accidental breaks. You can find fun patterns at many of your local home stores and online.

- Create a cozy setting by using an umbrella or small tent to construct an ideal space for dining.

- Candles, lanterns, and inexpensive lighting, such as white twinkle lights, can have the same effect, particularly in setting the stage for an evening meal.

- Big, bold blooms, like sunflowers placed in pitchers you already own, can make for centerpieces with lots of character. Go ahead and express yourself!

STYLE ISN'T ABOUT EXTRAVAGANCE, IT'S ABOUT DOING THE BEST WITH WHAT YOU HAVE

—MOLL

SUSHI
Sensation

SUSHI SENSATION

This table is often the one people decide to try first because it's fun, simple, and yet extremely exotic! Anyone can pick up sushi to go! It's the time and effort that goes into the sushi presentation that is important. Today, sushi is available not only in sushi restaurants, but in many other places, including your local grocery store, which makes sushi carry-out very convenient. You can also use Chinese or Thai food to create a similar vibe.

Creating your own Sushi Sensation does not have to be labor intensive. The flowers, for example, are a dozen beautiful red roses, which can also be found at your local grocery. Simply cut at the head of the rose and place among smooth river rocks atop the table; add lush green leaves from your garden and include three red glass hurricanes repurposed from the holiday season. Voilà, a cool and chic centerpiece! To complete this Asian theme, I added some fabulous plates, chopsticks, Saki, and cups. These items didn't cost a lot of money, but they really added to the overall ambiance.

If you don't have a dining room or you have limited space, don't despair! Think about using your coffee table and moving it to the center of your space. Throw a couple large pillows on either side of the table for a Japanese feel. You could string up a couple round Japanese paper lanterns in a color that correlates with your theme.

The idea is to create a getaway at home that allows you to take the time to relax and enjoy one another's company.

DECADENT *details*

When designing a theme dinner, the decadent details are truly what it's all about. The details tie everything together perfectly so you and your date feel like you have escaped to a faraway land, even though in reality you may just be steps from your back door. It starts when you begin to visualize the scene in your head and then translate it onto your table. The plates in this red motif, along with the napkins, rings and, of course, the chopsticks, were all essential in creating the Asian theme. I searched for the perfect Saki in a bottle that had great detail along with the Saki cups and carafe. The green edamame beans and leaves from the plants nearby all worked together with the river rocks to make for a perfect outdoor destination. The red roses brought a simple touch of elegance and a burst of passion to the scene. The tablecloth is actually a hand-woven shawl from the back of the kitchen chairs in our Santa Fe home—the perfect foundation for our Sushi Sensation.

FINDING YOUR MUSE

Ambiance is truly what I live for. It's all about the drama, baby! The fun kind of drama that makes your spouse or partner feel so special—because you created a theme that is intoxicating and über sexy. So I say step it up! All you need is twenty-four hours to truly make this unique kind of impression. If you don't have the lead-time, then take a scavenger hunt around your apartment or house. You would be amazed at how your imagination will be triggered when you zero in on something that will spark an idea for a theme.

For me it was my silver samurai statue. I grabbed him off a pile of books on an end table and decided to create a "Samurai Night." Once you have your theme in mind, make a list of the items you will need to gather to make your setting come to life.

- Take inventory of your dishes and china, crystal, silverware, placemats, tablecloths, napkins, etcetera. Take digital photos and place them in a folder on your phone or computer. Use your guide when shopping for details to enhance your tablescapes.

- Walk around your house in search of treasures that could become inspiration for your theme. Maybe items you picked up while traveling—shoot and file in your decadent details guide.

- Shop in your closet for clothing that you've either been dying to wear or happen to have from an old gala. Anything goes, from a sexy gown to a hula skirt!

- Search the web for inexpensive themed party goods and clothing. See resources on page 237.

- When you do a little planning ahead you will not only find the best deals but you will also incorporate a lot of what you already have.

PLANNING YOUR THEME

Music themes: Music can evoke memories of past events shared together. Bring the decades back to life with a music-based theme. Music from Frank Sinatra can bring alive the romance of '50s and '60s, or maybe create a disco theme event with music from the '70s. Center your table around that memory of a favorite song.

Seasonal inspiration: The change in seasons brings a new opportunity to celebrate with a table for two. Spring brings the emergence of beautiful flowers, and summer is the best time to plan a party for two under a star-filled night. And don't forget to harvest your own romance from the bounty of fall with warm, seductive colors from the changing leaves.

Food inspiration: Fresh, seasonal produce can inspire your theme. Fresh-from-the-garden vegetables can make for a salad soirée. Seasonal berries can inspire a champagne celebration or a delightful dessert-for-two picnic.

International flavors: From a taste of Italy to the seduction of France, bring your travel destinations and favorite flavors to your table theme.

PREPARATION AND ANTICIPATION OF A SIMPLE EVENING MAKES FOR A LUXURIOUS LIFE

—UNKNOWN

SANTA FE
Seduction

SANTA FE SEDUCTION

A summer afternoon in Santa Fe can be so inviting! Why? Because the weather is spectacular, the vibe in the air sings, and its spiritual qualities speak to the senses in every way imaginable. When Charlie and I arrive in Santa Fe, the first thing I like to do is head to the amazing farmers' markets for colorful homegrown veggies and fresh fruit. I'm always talking about spending your time wisely, so you can only imagine my excitement when grocery stores started roasting whole chickens (and doing it well). I felt like a brand-new world opened for me. Roasted chicken can be added to a variety of recipes, and while it might look as though you have been slaving for hours, you can whip up an amazing dinner with ease. This particular afternoon I was hoping to create a palette of food to make a hearty sandwich, one with fabulous bread slices of whatever he loves and condiments that add a little something unexpected.

DECADENT *details*

Planning a picnic is exciting because unlike the usual meal indoors at home, you get the chance to create an experience with the one you love in a new location. The key to preparing for a pleasurable excursion is in the decadent details. When dining alfresco, nature provides the backdrop, but it's up to you to build a sensory-scaped setting with the vibe you want. Layering for comfort, I threw together a ground mat, pillows, tablecloth, placemats, woven chargers, and napkins. For me, I wanted to make this lunch full of laid-back fun, so it was all about combining bright, bold colors with funky patterns and fabrics. Everything from the flowers to the food and sauces added a punch of color, and the details on the napkin rings and pillows made for an eclectically adorned adventure.

SUMMER SIPS

White wine is a refreshing incorporation to your summer celebrations. Choosing the right wine that satisfies your particular taste does not need to be difficult; there are no rules to pairing certain foods with wine anymore. Here are some popular wine choices that run from dry to sweet.

Chardonnay: Chardonnay is the most popular white wine. This wider-bodied dry white wine has subtle fruit flavors and often has a spicy or even buttery taste. It can be made sparkling or still.

Riesling: A very affordable sweet wine that is also available in dry varieties, Riesling originated in the river valleys of Germany from the Riesling grape. These wines have fruity aromas of apple, peach, and pear.

Pinot Grigio: Italy's most popular white wine, Pinot is a fairly dry and smooth wine, with hints of fruit from citrus to tropical flavors and ranging from melon to pear. Enjoy the flavor on its own or serve with appetizers, pasta, or fish.

Sauvignon Blanc: Originating in France, this crisp, refreshing medium-bodied wine offers a more herbal quality with the fruity flavors of sour apple, pear, and gooseberries. This wine can be found at a good value and works well with a variety of food choices.

LET'S GET DOWN

Creating a comfortable setting for your seductive picnic for two starts from the ground up. There are many more options available today that will make a meal on the go much more comfortable and easier to transport.

- Look for blankets, mats, and ground covers that roll up and fasten. These make transporting easier. Often these blankets are made with a waterproof underside, so there is no need to worry about where you settle your picnic spread.

- Old quilts, bedspreads, and throws will work for your outdoor meal, but consider a plastic ground cover between your quilt and the grass. Affordable plastic tablecloths and drop cloths will work for keeping your blanket dry.

- Try the cushion of a yoga mat under your throw. These will make for a softer, more comfortable placement and help level out the unevenness of the ground.

- No matter what you choose for the ground, don't forget to sensory-scape with big, oversized pillows. Bright colors and a variety of textures will add ambiance to any outdoor setting.

IF I HAD A FLOWER
FOR EVERY TIME
YOU MADE ME
SMILE
AND LAUGH, I'D HAVE
A GARDEN TO WALK IN
FOREVER

—UNKNOWN

TEA FOR *Two*

TEA FOR TWO

Take advantage of a beautiful, relaxing afternoon with an impromptu tea or cocktail for two. With a selection of fruits and cheeses on hand, I took advantage of some down time to host a quick and easy appetizer afternoon to refresh and reconnect with my husband. With a simple party-ready pantry and some basic bar essentials on hand, you can be ready when the time and opportunity arises. Even if you have not prepared for a last-minute soirée, use what you already have to create an impromptu afternoon. Sometimes the most memorable times happen in the moment, without any prior planning.

DECADENT *details*

Even though you may think of sweet tea as a southern tradition, I like to fuse my local favorites everywhere I go. Tex-Mex meals cooked in Tennessee, Santa Fe dinnerware in California, and foreign foods in any city—why not? Southern folks love their sweet iced tea; I can't even count the number of country songs written about it! So, in typical fashion, I played Southern hostess to my husband on the front porch. It all goes to show that you don't need an extravagant event. These fun wicker glasses and carafe complement the texture of our twig chairs and table. The special long matches, votives, quirky ring holders, and deeply colored sunflowers add the right amount of contrast to complete this sensory-scaped look. Soft furnishings invite relaxation, creating the perfect setting to sit and sip.

BEVERAGES

Nothing says summer like a glass of sweet tea. Spice up your tea for two by simply pureeing fresh fruit or nectar with fresh herbs, like mint, in a blender to add a flavorful punch to any basic tea.

Try some of these delicious options for adding fresh flavors to iced tea:

- Blackberry + lemon + mint
- Strawberry + sweet basil
- Raspberry + mint
- Watermelon (seedless) + mint
- Lemon + lime + lemon verbena
- Orange + thyme
- Blood orange + orange slice
- Try using flavored vodka in your late afternoon tea to spice up your tea time.

An easy way to add flavor to your tea is to add fresh fruits and herbs in your ice cube tray or muffin tin. Just add water and freeze. Muffin tins work well for freezing your icy treats, and the jumbo cubes last longer in your beverage on a hot summer day.

THE BAR NECESSITIES

The perfect home bar is unique for every seductive hostess and should reflect your and your partner's tastes. Stock your bar with your favorites. You might want to consider a special drink for your table for two celebration, or keep these staples on hand to enjoy together at the end of the day.

Barware: Old-fashioned glasses, high ball glasses, martini glasses, beer glasses (pilsner glasses or mugs)

Beverages:
- Liquors: vodka, gin, whiskey, rum, tequila, triple sec, scotch
- Wine: red and white
- Beer
- Mixers: tonic, soda water, ginger ale, cola, juices
- Sauces: Tabasco, Worcestershire, grenadine
- Garnishes: lemons, limes, mint, cherries, olives, cocktail onions

Extras:
- Toothpicks, stirrers
- Cocktail shakers
- Bottle opener, corkscrew
- Ice bucket and tongs
- Small paring knife, cutting board
- Slotted spoon, strainer, jigger
- Peeler, zester to make a citrus twist

EVEN TEA CAN BE AN APHRODISIAC... JUST ADD VODKA

—MOLL

LOVE

MAGICAL

WARMTH

SEDUCTIVE

CELEBRATIONS

I absolutely could not do this book without a celebration section! This is what it's all about. The truth is, Christmas and Hanukkah are the inspirations that the entire world uses to stop their crazy schedules just long enough to decorate specifically for this occasion. We plot, make lists, spend money we don't have, and stay up all night wrapping gifts! We bake and cook for days because either we have to or, even though we complain, we really love to. It's the one time a year our spaces are truly party ready. Why? Because we create ambiance. We go the extra mile. We drag all sizes of trees, living or fake, into our homes. We put thousands of lights and decorations all over the tree - and we don't stop the décor there. We decorate outside so everybody knows we have the holiday spirit. Take this same idea from the holiday season and create an environment that's celebration ready all year round, at the drop of a hat, when the mood strikes, when you have a babysitter! Christmas may be about the kids during the day, but the adults have the nights!

Moll

This is the season for you to step it up and have the time of your life! If you allow yourself to get excited about creating a celebration even for something simple, you will find yourself enjoying the moment and experiencing life and your relationship in a new and exciting way. My must-haves for chic and intimate celebrations are: glitz & glamour, presentation, atmosphere, whimsy, and deck the halls.

GLITZ & GLAMOUR—Celebrations should always be dramatically special no matter how small. Now is the time to let go and get a little HO-HO-Holiday crazy! Don't ever be afraid of going over the top—sometimes a surge of sparkle and extravagance will heighten your senses and transport you into a romantic fairytale full of glitz and glamour you've only been dreaming about.

PRESENTATION—Presentation is all in the decadent details. Set the tone of your seductive celebrations in the display of your gifts, décor, and tablescapes, and even in how you present yourself. From the wrapping paper that becomes an accessory, to your table setting or your holiday tree, to the way you wrap yourself up in your wardrobe as you wear the room beautifully—this is where you need to sparkle along with your room and table.

ATMOSPHERE—This is one of those times that there is truly no excuse for not creating a seductively festive setting. Atmosphere is everything! You can create any backdrop for any celebratory scene on any budget. This is not about breaking the bank; it's about making sure you create ambiance with the must-haves of lighting (with a simple dimmer switch), music, and flowers.

WHIMSY—Think beyond the typical affairs and add a touch of playfulness by incorporating unexpected, whimsical elements to your tablescape. Ornaments, treasures you've been saving, sweet nothings written on a note and wrapped up all hint of a merry evening. Whimsy is exhilarating and seductive.

DECK THE HALLS—Once you deck the halls, spend time with your family having fun, sharing food and drink, and fulfilling the traditions that make your family uniquely yours. But what's extremely important for you to remember is before you fall into bed exhausted, make sure that you celebrate with your partner in some special, seductive way.

GLITZ & GLAMOUR

DON'T EVER BE AFRAID OF GOING OVER THE TOP—A SURGE OF SPARKLE AND EXTRAVAGANCE WILL HEIGHTEN YOUR SENSES.

PRESENTATION

PRESENTATION IS ALL IN THE DECADENT DETAILS. SET THE TONE OF YOUR SEDUCTIVE CELEBRATIONS IN THE DISPLAY OF YOUR GIFTS, DÉCOR, AND TABLESCAPES, AND EVEN IN HOW YOU PRESENT YOURSELF.

ATMOSPHERE

ATMOSPHERE IS EVERYTHING! YOU CAN CREATE ANY BACKDROP FOR ANY CELEBRATORY SCENE ON ANY BUDGET.

WHIMSY

THINK BEYOND THE TYPICAL AFFAIRS AND ADD A TOUCH OF PLAYFULNESS BY INCORPORATING UNEXPECTED, WHIMSICAL ELEMENTS TO YOUR TABLESCAPE.

DECK THE HALLS

ONCE YOU DECK THE HALLS, SPEND TIME WITH YOUR FAMILY HAVING FUN, SHARING FOOD AND DRINK, AND FULFILLING THE TRADITIONS THAT MAKE YOUR FAMILY UNIQUELY YOURS.

Red Hot
VALENTINE

RED HOT VALENTINE

Valentine's Day for me is the Super Bowl of celebration! Valentine's Day is *the* one day of the year that couples are encouraged to show each other their feelings of love and appreciation and be romantic. My philosophy is to not celebrate your love on just one day; any day can be a celebration of your love for one another, and any meal can bring on the romance. While I love creating romantic soirées for two, I took this celebration up a notch with my King and Queen of Hearts theme and my beautiful, seductive heart-felt location.

Where did Valentine's Day begin? Actually, Valentine's Day came about because of one man's fight for love. Legend contends that Valentine, a priest during the third century in Rome, gave his life defending young love. Emperor Claudius II decided that unwed men were better soldiers than those with wives and families and outlawed marriage for them. Valentine, believing this law was unfair, betrayed Claudius and continued to marry young couples in secret. When his actions were revealed, Valentine was put to death and became forever a sacrifice of love. It is thought that right before his death Valentine sent an affectionate note to the beautiful daughter of his jailer and this was the very first valentine.

DECADENT *details*

Any day of the year is a time to celebrate your love, but for Valentine's Day I try to take things up a notch. I plan for this day in advance, setting the scene for my seductive table for two. For this table, I came up with the King and Queen of Hearts theme, and then scoped out a location for my table for two. With my vision in mind, I then searched for the decadent details to bring my Valentine's Day to life. After the holiday season, stores bring in a tremendous amount of red, pink, and love-themed decorations to stock for Valentine's Day. It is amazing the variety of valentine items that are available in January, and if you plan early enough, you can order your details online. I found hanging hearts and the fabulous themed pillows at a local craft store and reused the red fabric from a Christmas table, layering it with a crisp white cloth overlay. I planned my celebration mid-day to capture the warmth of the sun and followed up with a dinner for two in a cozy nook inside.

A TOUCH OF WHIMSY

Add a little touch of whimsy to your tablescapes and celebrations. Fun, whimsical, and even unexpected accents to your gatherings will help you get in touch with your playful side. It's easy to add these touches during holiday celebrations because there are so many festive decorations that are available both online and in the stores. But think beyond the holiday affairs and add playful touches to any tablescape.

Here are a few ideas:

- Let your imagination take flight with beautifully perched birds, birdcages filled with candles, floating feathers, birds' nests, and earthy elements tucked into your décor. Pull the look together with a light and airy color palette for a romantic and relaxed rendezvous.

- Find inspiration from books and movies! Forgotten favorites like *The Secret Garden*, *Alice in Wonderland*, and any adventure by Dr. Seuss will inspire you to create a fanciful fête for two.

- Bring on the spring and summer fun with brightly colored kites, confetti, hanging lanterns, fluffy paper pom-poms, and paper parasols or umbrellas that inspire child-like wonder and a carefree ambiance.

- Set a game night tablescape with your favorite classic game boards, such as Scrabble®, Monopoly, Clue®, dominoes, etc. Use the game board and player pieces for inspiration—Boardwalk anyone?

- Hang candles, votives, lights, and other decorations from trees and instantly transform a typical outdoor spot into a magical forest.

- Give your table a vintage flavor with old books, bottles, photos, and even an antique teapot with flowers. Mix vintage china pieces into your table setting.

Fun Fact: Have you ever wondered who the real Queen of Hearts was? She is believed by some to be a representation of Anne Boleyn, the second wife of Henry VIII. It has been suggested that the King of Hearts was Charlemagne, the King of Diamonds was Julius Caesar, the King of Clubs was Alexander the Great, and the King of Spades was the biblical King David.

CHOOSING CHINA

Whether you are single, newly married, or have an established home, a good set of china is an essential for entertaining.

- Purchase at least a five-piece place setting with a service for ten to twelve. This will allow you to be prepared for a seductive table for two or for an entire family gathering.

- You also don't have to confine yourself to one set of dinnerware. Having an everyday set and a fine set of china allows more flexibility in your use.

- Bone china and porcelain are the most beautiful, and they are also more chip resistant.

- A classic collection of white or cream dishes is a great choice because a more neutral plate will enhance the beauty of your food. White and cream china also make it easier in choosing linens, mixing plates, and for adding table accents.

- If you find some dinnerware you just love, purchase a set of two for your seductive table. Later mix and match your dishes for a fresh new look.

WHEN IN DOUBT, WEAR RED

—BILL BLASS

Delectable
DESSERTS

DESSERT NIGHT

Dessert night actually starts first thing in the morning—with sweet and simple love notes all written in matching stationery. I like to buy a little box of special notepaper with envelopes especially for the occasion. A pretty ink pen is always a nice touch. Write the cards in advance in order to have them ready to leave in special places that can be found throughout your lover's day. Maybe the first can be found in their briefcase or in the car attached to the steering wheel. The idea is to build excitement the entire day about what your partner can expect this particular and very special evening. Let your imagination run wild! Perhaps you meet at a little seductive restaurant for a dinner for two and then you hand the last note personally to them that suggests you go straight home for *dessert*!

Whatever you decide, just have fun and tap into your dating days when you felt your heart race and the anticipation of just being together was fantastic. Cakes, candy, chocolates, cookies, or cupcakes—whatever you serve will pale in comparison to you.

DECADENT *details*

Where I have a passion for spice, my husband's tooth is much sweeter, so his love of desserts is what inspired this surprise spread of sweets. Men are visual creatures, and the sense of sight is very powerful in enticing the taste buds. So I gathered an assortment of details that were flavorful and flirty, like cotton candy, Hershey's Kisses™, cakes, cookies, and even marshmallow kabobs. I sprinkled on the finishing touches, and the simple store-bought treats turned into decadent desserts by adding some pink icing and bright cupcake liners. I filled candy jars, topped cake stands, built a pyramid of cupcakes, and filled the counter space with bunched flowers as if they were giant gumballs to bring this flavorful fantasy to life. Before Charlie came home from work, I slipped into my new hot pink dress, turned down the lights, and turned on the music to make sure that the desserts were not the only thing he found delectable.

Fun Fact: A lollipop, which was invented by George Smith in 1908, was named after Lolly Pop, a racing horse.

SPARKLING FACTS

Champagne gets its name from the Champagne region of France where it was first created in the 1700s.

- There are different types of champagne: Brut is the driest and most popular, extra dry is less dry than Brut, and there are sweet champagnes labeled Sec and even sweeter Demi Sec.

- You will normally find champagne in dark glass bottles or wrapped in cellophane because the sensational liquid is very sensitive to light and UV rays' damaging effects.

- Drinking champagne from crystal champagne flutes is recommended because the tall and narrow design confines the bubbles, keeping them fresh longer, and focusing the aroma.

- The smaller the bubbles in sparkling champagne, the creamier and smoother it will taste in your mouth. Think: the smaller the bubbles, the more total bubbles, and more bubbles equal more flavor.

- Pink champagne was made famous in the film *An Affair to Remember* in which both of the lead actors fall in love and share their adoration for the pink bubbly. To make this rose champagne, creators let the grape skins soak with the liquid for a short time, and of course the longer it sits, the more pink your bubbly becomes.

SWEET TREATS

What makes a dessert night the perfect surprise is the combination of fun and fantasy. By shopping around, you can find all sorts of candies in tons of bright colors and flavors. Here I chose pink for a fun and flirty color scheme and incorporated everything I could find, from classic candies to bakery-bought confections.

- Choose an assorted mix of glass containers and cake stands to make a fun spread of sweets. These can be found very affordably in a variety of retail stores.

- Pick up desserts on the way home, and with a little food coloring and frosting you can add your own pop of color. All that is left to do is add sprinkles to make them sparkle.

- You don't have to be an Ace of Cakes to decorate your cupcakes. Instead of a pastry bag and decorator's tip, you can fill a plastic freezer bag with icing, leaving the top open, and simply cut off the tip of a bottom corner and swirl on your icing.

- You can mix store-bought frosting with half a container of Cool Whip for a quick, easy, and tasty alternative to homemade icing.

- Cupcake liners are a fun way to incorporate color and tie the treat into the theme.

EVERYBODY MUST HAVE A FANTASY, AND, PLEASE, MAKE SURE IT INVOLVES DESSERT

—MOLL

HOLIDAY
Elegance

HOLIDAY ELEGANCE

My "presentation is everything" philosophy carries over into my home, my style, and my life, and nothing speaks more to presentation than a beautifully wrapped gift.

Once you take the time to choose the right gift for someone, don't neglect the presentation. Your gift will feel all the more special because you have taken the time and effort to present a beautiful package. There are so many possibilities when wrapping a gift, from gift bags to decorative containers and boxes. Whatever you choose to hold your gift, remember to embellish it with decadent details. Get creative with wrapping paper, ribbon, and tags. Choose colors and patterns of paper and ribbon to coordinate with a theme or fit your décor, or make your selections to fit the recipient. Handmade tags, ornaments, photographs, or other small favors will add personal touches to your gifts.

DECADENT *details*

I love this time of year with all the beautiful selections for holiday decorations. With the sparkling lights, the abundance of ornaments, trims, ribbons, and bows, and the amazing tableware available for just this time, the decadent details abound. This time of year is when having a decadent detail guide will be so important; it will allow you to keep a record of all the holiday elegance you have chosen and stored all these years. When taking pictures of your special holiday details, keep a section of your guide for decadent details that can be repurposed for other celebrations in the off-season. In this table, the gold and white dinnerware, silverware, and linens can be used throughout the year for practically any occasion. The addition of chartreuse in the ribbons, ornaments, centerpiece, and glassware brings the holiday cheer to this table for two. The place cards and presents add a personalized touch to the holiday celebration of one another.

CELEBRATING EACH OTHER

The place card holder is certainly the star of this seductive holiday table for two. I love this glittering angular star ornament! I snipped the strings, arranged them on our plates, and ended up with a whimsical setting. Get imaginative and innovative when it comes to card holders! Trust me, you don't have to go out and buy anything to pull this fun setting together. Take a look around your home and try to see your belongings in a new light. Do you have a favorite ornament or novelty? Let it inspire you. If you just look at your trinkets from a different perspective, you may find you've already got a great card holder and just didn't realize it. These unique elements will lead you to an original table adorned with your own personal touches.

Fun Fact: Originally wallpaper was used for gift wrapping, but its thickness made folding difficult. Hallmark founder Joyce C. Hall actually stumbled into the invention of wrapping paper when a stack of decorative envelope lining papers from France were mistakenly set on top of the showcase and began to be sold as gift wrap!

PRESENT-ATION

What are your partner's favorite interests and passions? There are many creative ways to personalize a gift, outside the traditional wrapping paper and box.

- Use a map from your favorite vacation or a dreamed-about future destination.
- Newspaper is always an option to try—the sports section for the sports fanatic, or even the front page from an important date.
- Craft stores offer colorful archival boxes. Make copies of your favorite photographs and mementos and decoupage them on the box.
- Home improvement stores sell paint cans and buckets that can be filled with brightly colored tissue or shredded paper to hide the gift.
- Instead of wrapping a tie in a box, use his neckwear to wrap the box or other surprise.
- Chinese take-out boxes come in a variety of sizes and are easy to personalize.
- Themed gift baskets make for a great presentation. Just remember when wrapping a basket with cellophane or paper, use 3 times the size of the gift for the perfect amount of paper!

I WILL HONOR CHRISTMAS
IN MY HEART,
AND TRY TO KEEP IT
ALL THE YEAR

—CHARLES DICKENS

IL DESTINO DE A

HANUKKAH
Nightcap

HANUKKAH NIGHTCAP

While Christmas celebrates birth, the winter holiday of Hanukkah commemorates rebirth—the re-establishment of Jerusalem's historic second temple and the renewal of faith embraced by modern Jews worldwide.

According to the ancient story, when the Jews rededicated the holy temple, there was very little oil remaining to light the temple menorah (candelabra), since the bulk of the lamp oil had been polluted. But the oil they had, which was only enough for one day, miraculously lasted eight days. This is considered to be the origin of the eight-day celebration of Hanukkah, known as the "Festival of Lights." Similarly, the contemporary nine-branched Hanukkah menorah, also called a "chanukiah," is a tribute to the seven-branched, solid-gold candelabra used in the temple long ago.

Here, I was inspired by the traditional palette of blue and white seen in annual Hanukkah celebrations, a warm midnight blue well-complemented by the warmth of candlelight. Take one of these nights to celebrate the miracle of love between you and your partner. If you exchange gifts during these nights, maybe think about centering your theme on the gift you've given them. I encourage you to have fun with this evening, blending tradition with creativity! I used ornaments as napkin ring holders and added some glittering birds to an arrangement of white roses. Instead of a full-blown dinner, I also made this table a nightcap. A tray of desserts, fruit, and two glasses of wine set the tone for this elegant and meaningful night in.

IL DESTINO DE AMORE

DECADENT *details*

Cobalt blue and silver are such an incredibly exquisite combination. One dark, the other shining, together they capture both parts of the Hanukkah story: the destruction of the temple and the miracle of the candelabra oil. The moment you see this color duo, you feel the spirit of tradition that guides this eight-day remembrance. Here, I bring nature into the mix with a little pine entwined with silver-glittered ornamental vines, pheasant feathers, cobalt velvet, and sheer silk ribbon. A fire, a nightcap, and an intimate atmosphere offer a beautiful way to celebrate this holiday as well as your partnership with each other. Tradition is one of the many things I adore about the Jewish faith: rekindling connections to history, family, friends, and everything else that burns brightly in your life.

HANUKKAH GIVING

As you prepare to celebrate the Festival of Lights and embrace the tradition of the holiday, plan ahead to create some special moments with the people you cherish. Hanukkah offers eight nights of possibilities. Set aside one, perhaps the final evening, for just you and your partner to reflect on your time together.

If the two of you do not share the same faith, keep in mind that giving a gift for Hanukkah is not unlike choosing one for Christmas. What is meaningful to your partner? What do you know about their passions, their preferences, their unfulfilled dreams that would help you choose a gift?

Whether store-bought, homemade, or a combination of both, consider a gift...

...that sparks a memory of a treasured time: a framed picture, a memory box, or something as elaborate as recreating a first date.

...that may pique an emerging interest, such as a book on a specific topic, a magazine subscription, a private lesson, or tickets to a live event.

...based on a theme, and purchasing either one or all eight gifts guided by that theme.

...focused on charity: donating money and/or time in your partner's name for a worthwhile organization.

...in the form of a "love voucher," which they may redeem at any time.

...that pampers your partner with an experience, like a spa day or a massage, or else a comfort gift, like a cashmere throw, a sweater, a silk robe, or new bed linens.

...that supports your faith together.

Remember that presentation is an important part of gift-giving, so consider wrapping them in Hanukkah-themed paper or otherwise in the traditional colors of blue, white, and silver.

Fun Fact: The word *candle* is derived from the Latin word *candere*, meaning "to shine".

NIGHTCAPS AND CORDIALS

End your evening with a warm beverage to top off the day the right way.

- A nightcap is to be consumed in preparation for bedtime. Normally, the alcohol content in this type of beverage is higher than in a standard glass of wine or beer.

- Traditional nightcaps include brandy, bourbon, or cream-based drinks such as an Irish cream.

- People may often finish off their night with an abundantly sweet dessert drink, such as a port wine.

- Nightcaps often bring their drinkers a warm and fuzzy feeling right before bed, hypothetically putting a cap on the night.

- Non-alcohol drinkers normally treat themselves to a nice cup of decaffeinated coffee.

- Chamomile tea, an infusion of dried flowers, helps tea drinkers relax and get settled right before hitting the sheets. The tea itself induces a calming effect on the body.

COLORFUL CANDLES
BURNING BRIGHT,
EACH LIT
ON EIGHT VERY SPECIAL NIGHTS

—UNKNOWN

Holiday
GIVING TREE

HOLIDAY GIVING TREE

The holiday season is the perfect time to rekindle romance as you celebrate the spirit of giving. Making a difference by giving back and contributing to your community together can be extremely fulfilling and rewarding for your relationship. A shared goal is very powerful in feeling connected as a couple, so I encourage you to find a cause close to both of your hearts this season, and spend quality time working together in an act of service.

Spend your date night serving food at a local shelter or soup kitchen rather than going out for a meal. You could also bond with your partner as you prepare meals together to deliver to families in need. As a labor of love, join in on a local Habitat for Humanity build to provide shelter for a family. Or maybe in this year's holiday cards to family and friends, include a letter explaining your plans as a couple (shared holiday giving goal), and ask them to contribute in your honor and join with you by donating money, volunteering to build, or even helping to feed the volunteers. Who knows, you may even encourage other couples to create their own tradition of sharing the love.

Bring back the joy as you shop for toys and gifts together and adopt a child from the Angel Tree. Rather than putting dozens of gifts under the tree, you could decide to make it a family affair and pick a charity to which you all feel connected. Adopt a local family in need and give them a memorable Christmas this season. Have each member of your family select a member of the adopted family and meet up as a group at a selected store to shop together. Decide on a gift budget that works for everyone, then split up and shop for your designated family member. When you meet back, it is fun to not only see what gifts each of you has chosen, but you can really visualize the powerful impact your family will make on ones who are less fortunate.

There are so many incredible organizations that make a positive impact in the lives of others. Go with your heart and give the amazing gift that comes from true charity. During the season of indulgences, whether you decide to give money or time, giving together can reward your relationship and re-spark your romance as you remember how truly blessed you are to have one another during this special time of year.

DECADENT *details*

One of the many wonderful traditions of celebrating Christmas is adorning the tree with collections of found treasures and beautiful embellishments, and for me, the more the merrier. The decision to put up an artificial or living Christmas tree is a personal choice. The size of your tree selection is often influenced by where you place your tree and the scale of the room. If your tree is not as tall or as wide as you would like, you can change the scale with the decorations you choose. For artificial trees, you can fill in the gaps with extra tree branches or garlands purchased at craft and specialty stores. Once you have had your fill, so to speak, you can begin layering your decorations. I incorporated oversized details to my artificial tree to create a spectacular holiday tree and used a monochromatic color scheme. The full and billowing bows, long, fragile, blown-glass ornaments, and a flock of life-size white birds perched among the twinkling lights created the ideal essence required to bring this sunroom to life.

Seasonal
DECORATIONS

SEASONAL DECORATIONS

The magic and wonder of Christmas began when I was a little girl. My mom knew how to bring dazzle to the holiday, lighting the trees with big, bright, colorful bulbs. The tree filled our small space with its grand scale, and from this memory I create seasonal décor with the same wow factor that I cherished as a child. The tradition of selecting the tree together as a family is a treasured memory. My father, mother, brother, and I would go to the Christmas tree lot together to pick the perfect tree that would reside in our living room for weeks, or at least until the pine needles covered the carpet. We would spend hours browsing the tree lot until we all agreed we had found just the right one. Because I grew up in Scottsdale, Arizona, we were not bundled up, shivering in the December cold; we were in a Christmas tree lot surrounded by brown desert, green belts, mountains, and palm trees.

Over the years, my holidays were not always merry, but the memories of our family Christmases and our special trees motivated me to bring the wow factor to the Christmas tree every single year. I believe that my adversity has made me a really great designer because I have always seen the possibilities of creating something magical from the ordinary. I could look at a bin full of anything and immediately see it transformed into dazzling ornaments. Gold and silver spray paint would transform everything from plastic green grapes to branches from my yard, and then I would toss glitter all over them. I never let the holidays go by without the sparkle.

Today seasonal decorations for me are a blessing, a reminder and a testament to what seeing possibilities in your life can do!

DECADENT *details*

I strive for the same vibe and balance when choosing seasonal décor for a particular room in any home, but especially my own. I love when a room is perfectly balanced in color, shine, and warmth because it just feels right to your senses. You may not be able to put your finger on it, but you find yourself wanting to stay in the room longer; you feel cozier, sexier, and simply more luxurious. The decadent details in this particular room are the ultimate for a "Haute Holiday." The gold leaf on the ceiling shines down on the space and illuminates the tree, the gifts, the Italian plaster walls, and the painting. It is as though the sun is just about to set. It's so sensual. I love coordinating the gift wrap as an accessory to the room by using paper that looks as if you could roll it onto the walls as wallpaper. I choose different but gorgeous ribbons for each family member to make it easy for me to play Santa when we gather around to share in the Christmas spirit. It's so much fun to express yourself when you decorate your holiday trees. Let go and make magic!

TRADITION OF STOCKINGS
OVER THE CHIMNEY

"The stockings were hung by the chimney with care..." is a famous line from Clement Moore's Christmas poem, "Twas the Night Before Christmas." But have you ever wondered why we hang stockings? Although most countries have their own variations on Santa, the oldest reference to St. Nicholas goes as far back as the third century. One of the stories involves St. Nick passing by the homes of maidens who were too poor to afford a dowry (money that a bride gives to her groom for their wedding). The kind-spirited bishop would throw gold coins down the chimneys of these maidens, where they would fall into stockings, which were hung over the fire to dry.

In our home, we love having the tradition of stockings for all our kids and now our granddaughter. The difference is they are not filled with gold coins. We fill the stockings with fun items that don't cost a lot of money but everyone loves and counts on getting. For girls, you might think about getting the new trend in lip gloss and nail polishes or fun bangles and earrings. For guys, think cufflinks, socks, lip balm, and CDs. The idea is that no matter how small the gift, it gets wrapped completely. The whole family gets to take their time unwrapping and spending more quality time together.

DECADENT *details*

Every single family has its very own special Christmas traditions, from the ornaments on the tree to the stockings that hang with each name lovingly embroidered on the cuff. The decadent details are unique to every single person in every home across the world, and that's why they are remarkable. You may hang little twinkling white lights or oversized multi-colored strands. My signature style is to find the biggest tree possible and place it in our great room. Our tree is artificial, but to keep my husband from not missing a real tree, we tie in live greens picked up from the tree lots. Pre-lit trees are so easy to use, with thousands of twinkling bulbs already hung and without all the hassle. I also tuck hand-painted amber lights into each section of the tree for a warm glow. Crimson cardinals, shimmering ornaments, and hand-blown glass balls perfect this tree when added with over-the-top large ornaments in hues of gold and red. I place red poinsettias throughout the house to achieve the most classic of holiday impressions. These bold plants are inexpensive and will last you throughout the season.

HOSTESS GIFTS

In place of a traditional hostess gift, share the love and give your friends something that encourages them to romance their partners.

- Holiday spirits: Instead of just a bottle of wine or liqueur, add a pair of matching glasses.
- Candles: *Every* room should smell good during the holidays, so give a set of votive candles that match their bedroom instead of a set of traditional holiday-scented candles.
- Breakfast-in-bed basket: Include various jams, baguettes, croissants, scones, or bagels, fresh fruit, coffee beans/grinds, and tea bags so that after a long evening of entertaining, there are no worries the morning after.
- Fireside: Gift some gourmet hot cocoa, two matching mugs, and a plush, warm blanket so they can snuggle by the fire.
- Seductive sounds of the season: Give the gift of music with a romantic and relaxing seasonal compilation that they can enjoy together while winding down.
- Meal for two: Give your hostess a night off from cooking with everything needed for a meal for two—gourmet pasta, sauces, infused olive oils, balsamic vinegar—wrapped in a beautiful bowl or serving dish.

CHRISTMAS WAVES ITS
MAGIC WAND
OVER THIS WORLD AND BEHOLD,
EVERYTHING'S SOFTER AND
MORE BEAUTIFUL

—NORMAN VINCENT PEALE

AROMA

SAVORY

SPICY

SEDUCTIVE
RECIPES FOR TWO

How better to express yourself than with a meal prepared for the one you love. I love to cook meals that look just as fabulous as they taste. Plated food is an art that should be savored. Life is busy and time is a great luxury, so I look for simple ways to get a meal on the table. Although picking up food to take home works well with a fabulous presentation, it's fun to enjoy the sensuality of preparing a meal. My Seductive Recipes "for Two" includes "time-saving" recipes and even my personal favorites. I have included quick morning delights to indulge in right in bed, lunch ideas to pack in a picnic, and dinner recipes that are sure to please the heart of the one that you love. Sip into Seduction with my beverages and cocktail recipes. Create desserts that will curl your toes and make your taste buds tingle. It's all meant to encourage you to have fun and find delight in the process. Pour a glass of wine, put on your playlist, and prepare to dazzle yourself and the one you love.

Moll

MORNING
recipes for two

PRALINE TO A KISS

A little treat in the morning makes for a special start to the day.

TOAST

4 (1-inch) slices French bread
Butter for the baking dish
2 eggs
$\frac{1}{2}$ cup half-and-half
$\frac{1}{4}$ cup milk
$\frac{1}{4}$ cup sugar
2 teaspoons vanilla extract
$\frac{1}{8}$ teaspoon cinnamon
$\frac{1}{8}$ teaspoon nutmeg
Dash of salt

TOPPING

4 tablespoons butter ($\frac{1}{2}$ stick)
$\frac{1}{4}$ cup packed light brown sugar
$\frac{1}{4}$ cup pecans
2 teaspoons light corn syrup
$\frac{1}{8}$ teaspoon cinnamon

Arrange the bread in a generously greased 9-inch square baking pan or loaf pan, overlapping the slices slightly.

Beat the eggs, half-and-half, milk, sugar, vanilla, cinnamon, nutmeg and salt in a bowl until well blended. Pour the mixture over the bread. Cover with aluminum foil. Refrigerate for at least 8 hours.

Melt the butter in a small saucepan or bowl. Add the brown sugar, pecans, corn syrup, and cinnamon and mix well. Spoon the mixture over the soaked bread. Bake at 350 degrees for 40 minutes until golden. For a luxe, decadent breakfast, serve with a lashing of maple syrup. Serves 2.

GET LEI'D HAWAIIAN FRENCH TOAST

4 (1-inch) slices Hawaiian bread
½ cup heavy cream
2 eggs
½ teaspoon cinnamon
¼ teaspoon vanilla extract
1 to 2 tablespoons confectioners' sugar
Fresh lemon juice
Berries

Heat a griddle or skillet to medium (350 degrees). Beat the cream, eggs, cinnamon, and vanilla in a wide bowl. Dip each slice of bread into the egg mixture. Coat the griddle with nonstick cooking spray. Cook the toast for 3 to 4 minutes on each side until browned.

Sift confectioners' sugar over the toast. Squeeze a few drops of lemon juice on each slice. Serve with fresh berries. Serves 2.

MORNING QUICKIE

Fast, healthy and portable!

Nonstick cooking spray
½ cup egg substitute (or 2 eggs)
1 teaspoon water
2 to 4 tablespoons chopped ingredients (see below)
2 tablespoons shredded cheese (see below)

Spray a large mug or ramekin with non-stick cooking spray. Combine the eggs and other ingredients in the mug. Microwave on high for 1 minute. Stir the mixture, then microwave 30 to 45 seconds until set. Serve immediately.

Greek Mug—spinach, artichoke hearts, and feta

Mexican Mug—black beans, corn, peppers, tomatoes, Mexican-blend cheese. Top with salsa or garnish with guacamole.

Meaty Mug—sausage, bread crumbs or croutons, and cheese

Italian Mug—basil, tomato, and mozzarella

SALSA ME BACK TO BED

Just like huevos rancheros, the Mexican classic, but in half the time.

2 to 4 corn tortillas
1 (8-ounce) jar chunky medium-hot salsa
1 (8-ounce) can tomato sauce
4 to 6 eggs
Chopped fresh cilantro
Sliced avacado

Wrap the tortillas in foil. Heat in a 300-degree oven while preparing the toppings. Combine the salsa and tomato sauce in a 10-inch skillet. Bring to a simmer; cook for 5 minutes. Crack the eggs into the salsa. Cover the skillet and cook for 5 minutes for soft-set, 7 minutes for fully-cooked yolks. Arrange a tortilla or two on each plate. Top with eggs. Spoon sauce over the eggs. Sprinkle with cilantro and garnish with avacado. Serves 2.

EGG-CITE ME

Mild and flavorful green chiles line a baking dish, and get a topping of cheese and eggs.

- 1 (4-ounce) can whole green chiles
- ½ cup shredded Monterey Jack cheese
- Salt and pepper to taste
- 4 eggs
- ⅓ cup half-and-half, cream, or evaporated milk
- Salsa and sour cream for serving

Preheat the oven to 350 degrees. Slit the chiles lengthwise and remove the seeds. Pat dry. Grease a 7-inch loaf pan or small (7-inch) baking dish, or two mini loaf pans. Open the chiles flat and arrange them, skin side down, in the dish. Top with cheese. Season with salt and pepper. Beat the eggs and cream in a bowl. Pour over the cheese layer.

Bake for 45 minutes until center is set. Let stand for 5 to 10 minutes. Cut into squares. Serve with salsa and sour cream. Serves 2.

SEDUCTIVE WAKE-UP CALL

FOR EACH OMELET

- 1 teaspoon olive oil
- 1 tablespoon chopped serrano chile
- 1 teaspoon chopped fresh cilantro
- 2 eggs or 3 egg whites, or ½ cup egg substitute
- 1 twist of sea salt from a grinder
- 2 twists of pepper from a grinder
- 2 tablespoons goat cheese, feta, or Monterey Jack cheese
- 3 pieces applewood-smoked bacon, cooked and crumbled
- ½ avocado, cut into slices lengthwise
- Salsa and Tabasco, for serving

Make one omelet at a time, or make two side by side if you have two omelet pans.

Heat the oil in a small omelet pan. Sauté the chiles and cilantro briefly. Add the eggs, sea salt, and pepper. Cook, lifting the edge of the omelet and tilting the pan so the uncooked egg flows underneath. Cook to desired doneness. Flip the omelet over or broil briefly to cook the top.

Add the cheese, bacon, and avocado. Slide the omelet onto a plate, folding it over the filling.

Fun Fact: The rumor that adding milk to eggs will make them fluffy, is just that—a rumor. Milk actually binds the yolks making them heavier. For fantastically fluffy scrambled eggs, add a teaspoon or more of water while beating. Do this when beating egg whites for omelets and you may find the volume will practically double.

UNDER LOX AND KEY

For a quick and easy breakfast, pick up lox at the market. No delicatessen nearby, no problem: it's easy to make your own gravlax.

- 1 (8-ounce) salmon fillet, skin on or off
- 1 tablespoon salt
- 1 tablespoon sugar
- 1/2 teaspoon coarsely ground black pepper
- 2 tablespoons chopped fresh dill (including stems)
- Pinch of red pepper flakes, optional
- 1/2 teaspoon caraway seeds, optional
- 2 tablespoons bourbon, vodka, or scotch

Set the salmon in a small glass baking dish, skin side down. Combine the salt, sugar, and red pepper. Rub the mixture into the salmon. Spread the dill, pepper, and caraway over the fish, pressing them into the flesh. Sprinkle with the bourbon.

Cover with plastic wrap. Top with a couple pounds of weights (canned goods work well). Refrigerate for 24 to 48 hours. Scrape off most of the seasoning. Use a very sharp knife held at an angle to cut very thin slices diagonally. Serve with Luxe Spread on bagels or toast. Keeps for up to three days in the refrigerator. Serves 2.

LUXE SPREAD

I love puréed herbs packaged in a tube, found in the refrigerated produce section of the supermarket. They're great for recipes like this, which use just a touch of parsley. No mincing and no waste!

- 4 ounces (about 1/2 block) cream cheese, softened
- 1/4 teaspoon lemon zest
- Few drops of lemon juice
- 1 teaspoon sliced green onion tops
- 1 teaspoon capers
- 1/4 teaspoon caper juice
- 1 teaspoon chopped fresh parsley (or a little parsley puree from a tube)

Combine all of the ingredients in a small bowl with a fork. Makes 8 tablespoons.

PLEASURE PARFAITS

Fresh and light, a parfait is a good breakfast solution for a sleepy appetite.

| 1 cup grapes (cut into halves), berries, pitted cherries, or sliced banana
| 12 ounces lemon or vanilla yogurt
| 1 cup granola

Layer half of the fruit in two parfait, wine, or pilsner glasses, dividing it evenly between them. Spoon about 3 ounces of yogurt over the fruit. Add another layer of fruit, using the remaining amount.

Top with the 3 more ounces of yogurt on each parfait. (You can prepare the parfaits to this point and refrigerate them for 8 hours.) Top each with ½ cup granola right before serving. Serves 2.

MEAT ME FOR BREAKFAST

BÉARNAISE SAUCE

¼ cup (½ stick) butter
1 cup milk
1 envelope McCormick béarnaise sauce mix

EGGS AND ASSEMBLY

4 large eggs
2 filets mignons, cooked
2 English muffins, split

For the sauce, melt the butter in a small saucepan over medium-low heat. Stir in the milk, and whisk in the sauce mix. Cook over medium heat, stirring frequently, until sauce comes to a boil. Lower to a simmer and cook for 1 minute, stirring, until thickened.

For the eggs, half-fill a skillet with water. Bring to a simmer. Break the eggs into buttered egg cups, or poach directly in the water for 2 to 3 minutes. Remove the skillet from the heat but leave the eggs in the water.

Warm the meat. Toast the muffins. Set a filet on each of two muffin halves. Drain the eggs and dab them dry. Set two eggs on each filet. Top with béarnaise sauce. Serves 2.

BUTTER ME UP

Get scones from your favorite bakery, or bake frozen croissants. Serve them with one or more of these enticing butters.

The better the butter, the better the flavor. Pick a premium butter such as Kerry Gold or PluGra for the finest flavor and texture.

BERRY BUTTER

½ cup (1 stick) butter, softened
½ cup strawberries, blueberries, blackberries or raspberries

Beat the butter in a small bowl with an electric mixer (or use a food processor) until creamy. Add the berries and beat for 3 to 4 minutes until well combined. Use right away, or spoon into a glass or ceramic container and refrigerate until firm. Makes 4 servings.

ORANGE BUTTER

½ cup (1 stick) butter, softened
Zest of 1 orange

Beat (or process) the butter and orange zest until well combined. Use right away, or spoon into a glass or ceramic container and refrigerate until firm. Makes 4 servings.

MAPLE BUTTER

½ cup (1 stick) butter, softened
3 tablespoons maple syrup

Beat (or process) the butter and syrup until very well blended. This mixture is thin and should be refrigerated for an hour to firm up (unless you're using it for pancakes). Makes about 5 servings.

MAGIC MUFFINS

These muffins are little miracles! High in fiber, with a chocolatey taste, they mix up quickly and can be baked in the oven or microwave.

- $1/2$ cup bran stick cereal
- 1 cup chocolate Cheerios
- $3/4$ cup boiling water
- 2 tablespoons butter, melted
- 1 tablespoon dark, unsweetened cocoa powder
- 1 cup buttermilk
- $3/4$ cup sugar
- $1^1/2$ cups unbleached flour
- 1 teaspoon baking soda
- $1/4$ teaspoon salt

Combine the cereals and boiling water in a medium bowl. Let stand for 20 minutes—mixture will be thick and pasty. Mix the butter and cocoa. Add to the cereal mixture, along with the buttermilk. Add the sugar, flour, soda, and salt and mix well.

Refrigerate the mixture in a tightly covered container for at least 8 hours. To bake muffins, scoop $1/2$ cup into a well-greased microwave-safe mug. Microwave one muffin at a time for $1^1/2$ minutes (for a 1100-watt oven).

Or bake the mixture in a greased muffin tin, or in cupcake liners, at 350 degrees for 25 minutes. Makes 8 to 9 muffins.

The batter keeps two weeks in the refrigerator—maybe longer, but they never last long enough for us to find out!

PUMP-KIN ME UP

- 2 cups milk (can substitute 1 cup of half-and-half for thicker consistency)
- 4 tablespoons sweetened condensed milk
- 4 tablespoons pumpkin puree
- $1/2$ teaspoon pumpkin pie spice
- $1/2$ teaspoon vanilla extract
- 8 tablespoons double strength brewed coffee

GARNISH:

Whipped cream
Pumpkin pie spice
Cinnamon stick

Combine milk, sweetened condensed milk, pumpkin, spice and coffee in a saucepan; whisk thoroughly and bring to nearly boiling. Remove from heat and stir in vanilla.   Garnish with whipped topping, dash of pumpkin pie spice, and a cinnamon stick. Serves 2.

HOT AND STEAMY

Warm, soothing, and just sweet enough. Add a splash of coffee if that strikes your fancy.

| 2 cups milk
| 2 to 3 tablespoons Toroni vanilla syrup
| Dash of nutmeg

Combine the milk and syrup in a quart-size glass jar. Microwave on high for 2 minutes. Pick up the jar with a hot pad or oven mitt, and put on a lid and tighten it. Shake the jar very hard for at least 30 seconds. (Or transfer the mixture to a blender and blend on high for 30 seconds to 1 minute.) Pour into 2 mugs. Add a dash of nutmeg. Serves 2.

SMOOTHIE OPERATOR

The bold flavor is a great "wake-me-up."

| 1½ cups diced fresh pineapple
| 1 banana
| ½ cup plain or vanilla Greek yogurt
| 1 tablespoon grated fresh ginger or 1 teaspoon ground
| dried ginger
| ½ cup ice
| ½ cup pineapple juice
| Dash of cinnamon

Combine all of the ingredients in a blender. Process until smooth. Serve immediately. Serves 1 or 2.

MARRY ME MINT-MOSA

| 1 cup fresh orange juice
| 2 tablespoons confectioners' sugar
| 4 mint leaves
| ¼ teaspoon freshly grated lime zest
| Champagne

Combine the orange juice, sugar, mint leaves, and lime zest in a blender. Pour (or strain) into 2 glasses. Top with champagne. Serves 2.

RED HOT BLOODY MARY

| ½ cup chile-infused vodka (page 222)
| 2 cups Zing Zang Bloody Mary Mix
| Ice
| Lime wedges

Combine the vodka and Bloody Mary mix in a pitcher. Fill 2 large glasses with ice. Pour in the Bloody Mary. Add a squeeze of lime. Serves 2.

FRISKY CHICK

2 large, boneless, skinless chicken breasts
Salt and pepper to taste
1 teaspoon minced garlic
2 tablespoons olive oil
$^3/_4$ teaspoon Italian seasoning
Sea salt and freshly cracked black pepper
4 ounces soft, mild goat cheese, at room temperature
2 ounces cream cheese, at room temperature
$^1/_4$ cup Presto Pesto (recipe page 205)
$^3/_4$ cup mixed greens
Balsamic vinegar to taste
2 slices red bell pepper
2 ciabatta rolls, split in half, warmed

Season the chicken with salt and pepper. Combine with the garlic, olive oil, and Italian seasoning in a bowl. Marinate for at least 1 hour, or refrigerate for 8 hours.

Blend the goat cheese, cream cheese, and pesto in food processor until smooth. Season to taste with salt and pepper.

Remove the chicken from marinade and season again with salt and pepper. Grill over high heat for about 4 minutes per side until cooked through.

Toss the mixed greens with balsamic vinegar. Spread the rolls with the goat cheese mixture. Top with chicken, red bell pepper, and a handful of the dressed greens. Top with the other half of the roll.

Refrigerate the remaining cheese spread. Serves 2.

PRESTO PESTO

Chicken, pasta, fresh mozzarella—pesto is a delicious accompaniment to all of them, and lots more besides.

2 cups packed fresh basil leaves
1/2 cup freshly grated Parmesan or romano cheese
2 garlic cloves, minced
1/4 cup toasted pine nuts
1/2 cup extra virgin olive oil
Sea salt and pepper to taste

Combine the basil, cheese, garlic, and nuts in a food processor. Pulse a few times. With the motor running, drizzle in the oil gradually. Process until well blended. Season with salt and pepper.

Pesto freezes well—just pour a little oil over the top before sealing. Use within 3 months for the best flavor.

SEDUCE ME SANTA FE

CHICKEN SALAD

2/3 cup sour cream
3 tablespoons lime juice
1/2 teaspoon salt
1/4 teaspoon black pepper
1/4 teaspoon paprika
1/4 teaspoon cumin
1 to 2 tablespoons minced cilantro
2 to 3 green onions, thinly sliced
1 celery rib, minced

2 cups shredded poached chicken
2/3 cup cooked or canned black beans
1/3 cup minced red bell pepper
1/3 cup corn kernels

WRAP AND ASSEMBLY

Salad greens or baby spinach
Large flour tortillas
Avocado slices
Salsa, for serving

For the chicken salad, combine the sour cream, lime juice, salt, pepper, paprika, cumin, and cilantro in a medium bowl and mix well. Add the green onions, celery, and chicken and mix well. Fold in the black beans, bell pepper, and corn. Cover and chill until ready to serve.

For the wraps, layer chicken salad, salad greens or baby spinach, and avocado slices on the tortillas. Fold up the ends and roll the wrap to enclose the filling. Slice in half. Serve with salsa on the side, if desired. Makes 4 cups chicken salad, about 4 servings.

ARTICHOKE AFFAIR

2 large artichokes
6 to 8 garlic cloves, peeled
2 lemons, cut into quarters
Olive oil
Cracked black pepper to taste
Salt to taste
Sugar
Salt and pepper

Melted butter, aged balsamic vinegar, mayonnaise, hollandaise sauce, aioli, Dijon-spiked plain yogurt or lemon juice for dipping.

Trim the stems of the artichokes so they are flat and level, or cut them off flush with the base. Cut off the top 1 to 2 inches of prickly leaves with a serrated knife. Stuff 3 or 4 peeled garlic cloves inside and around the top of the artichokes. Squeeze the lemon wedges over the artichokes (save the squeezed wedges). Drizzle with olive oil, and sprinkle with pepper.

In a large saucepan deep enough for the artichokes, stand them upright, using the lemon wedges to support them. Add enough water to reach 2 inches up the artichokes. Add a little salt and a dash of sugar to the water (these help preserve the color and flavor). Cover the pot and bring to a simmer. Simmer for 45 minutes to 1 hour.

Drain the artichokes. Stand them upside down in a bowl to drain thoroughly. Let them cool a little.

To eat, pull the leaves off one at a time. Dip into butter, mayonnaise, hollandaise, or other dip. Scrape the leaf between your top and bottom teeth to get the rich flesh on the bottom of the leaf. Discard the remaining tough upper part of the leaf.

When you get to the light-colored inner leaves, you can pull them all out at once, bite off the tender base, and then discard the remainder. Do not eat the "choke," the fuzzy center of the artichoke. Remove the choke by stroking with a fork, or cut it out with a small paring knife. This will leave the base of the artichoke, the most delicious part. Serves 2.

TAIL ME WHAT YOU WANT

To make the best shrimp cocktail, you need the freshest shrimp. Feel the shrimp if possible—fresh shrimp are firm and dry.

> Buy the right amount: 2 pounds of shrimp yields about 1 pound of cooked, shelled shrimp, or 2 cups.

It's a good idea to devein shrimp. There are several ways to do this—the most straightforward is to peel the shrimp, then run a knife down the center back of each shrimp. (There are other methods, including using a two-tined fork, that take practice but work well. Search YouTube for how-to videos, and keep practicing!)

Use a little shrimp boil seasoning in the water to flavor the shrimp. Or create your own by adding lemons, bay leaves, pepper flakes, onions, salt, and pepper to 10 cups of water. Let it boil 10 minutes to fully develop the flavor. Scoop the lemons and bay leaves out with a slotted spoon before adding the shrimp.

Cook the shrimp just until they turn pink, about 2 minutes, then drain them right away. Run cold water over them to stop the cooking. Cool slightly. Serve warm, or refrigerate for chilled shrimp.

Serve with Skinny Dippin' or Getta Room-oulade.

SKINNY DIPPIN'

Just four ingredients, and the food processor does the rest. Take along Skinny Dippin' on a picnic as a dip for corn chips, or use it as a different dunk for shrimp cocktail. It's also excellent for topping fish tacos (page 215).

> 1/4 cup Herdez brand salsa verde (from an 8-ounce can), or more to taste
> 1 avocado, pitted
> Juice of 1/2 lime (about 1 tablespoon)
> 1 scant handful cilantro
> Salt and pepper to taste

Combine the salsa, avocado, lime juice, cilantro, salt and pepper in a food processor or blender. Process until the avocado is puréed. Makes 1 cup.

GETTA ROOM-OULADE

A dunk for chilled shrimp or a spread for tomato sandwiches— the flavors here can liven up a lot of dishes.

> 1/2 cup mayonnaise
> 1 cup arugula leaves
> 1 tablespoon capers
> 1/8 teaspoon cayenne pepper
> 1 tablespoon fresh lemon juice
> Salt to taste

Combine all the ingredients in a food processor. Pulse until the arugula and capers are finely chopped. Makes about 3/4 cup.

LAYERS OF LOVE—WATERMELON SALAD

LEMON MINT YOGURT DRESSING

> 1/2 cup plain Greek yogurt
> 1/4 teaspoon lemon zest
> 2 tablespoons lemon juice
> 1/4 teaspoon salt
> 1 teaspoon chopped fresh mint (or crushed dried mint)

SALAD

> Watermelon, cut into 1/2-inch cubes
> Feta cheese, cut into small cubes
> Greek black olives, pitted, torn
> Very thinly sliced red onion
> Romaine lettuce, torn into bite-size pieces

Combine the dressing ingredients in a small bowl. Whisk to blend. Divide the dressing evenly between 2 pint-size wide-mouth canning jars. Layer the watermelon, then the feta cheese, a few olives and onion to taste. Top with layers of lettuce and feta cheese. When ready to serve, turn upside down or shake to coat the ingredients with dressing. Serves 2.

LAYERS OF LOVE—ASIAN SALAD

You can lightly steam the sugar snap peas or leave them uncooked, whichever you prefer.

GINGER DRESSING:

3 tablespoons grated fresh ginger
¼ cup vegetable oil
3 tablespoons soy sauce
2 to 3 tablespoons brown sugar
1 teaspoon lime or orange juice
½ teaspoon minced serrano chile

SALAD

½ cup sugar snap peas or snow peas, sliced
½ cup shredded purple cabbage
2 green onions, sliced
½ cup cucumber slices
Alfalfa sprouts, spicy sprouts, or bean sprouts
2 tablespoons chopped toasted almonds
½ cup torn romaine lettuce

For the dressing, combine the dressing ingredients in a bowl with a whisk, or shake in a jar with a tight-fitting lid.

For the salads, pour about 2 tablespoons of the dressing into each of two quart-size, wide-mouth canning jars. Add a layer of sugar snaps, dividing them evenly between the jars. Repeat with the cabbage, green onions, cucumber, and sprouts. Top with a layer of lettuce. Fit the lids on the jars and tighten the rings.

When ready to serve, turn the jars over to coat the vegetables with dressing. Serves 2.

LAYERS OF LOVE—ANTIPASTO SALAD

½ cup giardiniera (Italian pickled vegetables)
½ cup small mozzarella balls
½ cup pitted kalamata olives
2 tablespoons capers
6 to 8 thin slices of sopressata or other hard salami
½ cup marinated artichoke hearts

Remove the lids from two clean quart-size wide-mouth canning jars. Layer the ingredients in order, dividing them evenly between the jars. Put on the lids and tighten the rings. Refrigerate to chill if desired, though this salad is safe at room temperature for several hours. Serves 2.

TAKE ME TO MOROCCO

Serve this sensuously spiced burger on a bun or go naked.

- 8 ounces ground round
- 2 small shallots, coarsely chopped
- 2 tablespoons chopped cilantro
- 2 tablespoons chopped flat-leaf parsley
- 2 tablespoons chopped fresh mint or 2 teaspoons dried mint
- 1 garlic clove, minced
- 1/2 teaspoon ground cumin
- 1/2 teaspoon ground coriander
- 1 small red or green chile, deseeded, chopped
- 1/8 teaspoon ground allspice

SAUCE

- 1/4 cup crumbled feta cheese
- 1/4 cup plain Greek yogurt
- 1 tablespoon chopped fresh mint

Put the meat in a bowl. Sprinkle all of the remaining ingredients evenly over the meat. Mix with a fork or your hands to combine. Shape into burgers. Grill, broil, or pan-fry to desired doneness.

Combine the sauce ingredients in a small bowl. Spoon over the burgers. Serves 2.

EASY CAPRESE

- 8 ounces ground round
- 2 slices Buffalo mozzarella
- 3 tablespoons Presto Pesto (page 205)
- 2 tomato slices
- Balsamic vinegar
- Fresh basil

Place meat in bowl. Add 2 tablespoons Presto Pesto. Mix with a fork or your hand to combine. Form into patties and grill or broil burgers to your liking. Toast or grill bun. Spread remaining pesto on bun, then add hamburger, tomato, and mozzarella. Sprinkle with balsamic vinegar. Garnish with fresh basil.

RAJIN' CAJUN

Combine 8 ounces of ground beef with 4 ounces coarsely chopped spicy andouille. Season with salt and pepper to taste. Broil, grill or pan-fry to an internal temperature of 160 degrees. Spread mayonnaise on the buns. Sprinkle with a little cayenne pepper. Add the burgers.

HEADIN' SOUTH

Top your best burger with a few pickle slices, a tablespoonful of pimento cheese, and a piece of crisp-cooked smoked bacon.

HOT DIGGITY DOG BAR

Walk your favorite brand of hot dog and premium-quality buns through one of these great combinations. Good dog!

PERROS CUBANOS (CUBAN DOGS)

1/4 cup very thinly sliced red onion
Juice of 1 lime
1/2 teaspoon hot sauce
2 hot dog buns
2 slices Swiss cheese
2 cooked hot dogs
Sliced dill or sour pickles
Spicy brown mustard

Combine the onion, lime, and hot sauce in a small bowl. Let stand at least 15 minutes.

Split the buns. Top with Swiss cheese. Toast or broil for 3 minutes until the bun is warm and the cheese melts. Add the hot dogs, pickles, brown mustard, and the marinated onions.

HAWAIIAN DOGS

Nestle the hot dogs all the way down into the buns—you'll need the room at the top for this luscious combination of toppings. Spoon on chopped pineapple tidbits, Lawry's Hawaiian marinade, mustard, and Braswell's sweet Vidalia onion relish.

PIMENTO CHEESE DOGS

Top your eagerly awaiting hot dog with a tablespoon or two of prepared pimento cheese, prepared coleslaw, and sliced dill or sour pickles.

MUFFULETTA DOGS

Split two hot dog buns. Top with provolone cheese. Toast, broil, or microwave for a minute or two until cheese is melted. Spread a spoonful of olive tapenade on each bun. Add the hot dogs. Top with a layer of giardiniera.

RELISH ME

Try these flavored-up condiment ideas for burgers, hot dogs, and sandwiches—and whatever else you dream up!

Improvised Remoulade: Add 1 teaspoon capers, 1 teaspoon fresh lemon juice, some chopped parsley and several dashes of hot sauce to 1/2 cup Thousand Island dressing for an improvised Remoulade sauce.

Hot and sweet mayo: Stir 1 tablespoon of wasabi paste into 1/2 cup mayonnaise. Finely chop about 6 bread-and-butter pickle slices. Stir into the mayonnaise.

Pesto mayo: Stir 1 tablespoon of Presto Pesto (page 205) into mayonnaise.

Horseradish cream: Combine 2 tablespoons prepared horseradish and 1/2 cup sour cream. Add salt to taste.

Pickled mustard: Cut 2 well-drained pickled okra into thin slices. Combine with coarse mustard or honey mustard.

Curry ketchup: Stir 2 teaspoons mild curry powder into 1/2 cup ketchup. Serve with grilled hot dogs or brats for a German-style currywurst.

Buffalo mayo: Combine equal parts crumbled blue cheese and mayonnaise. Add a little cayenne pepper or hot sauce.

SUGAR LIPS

Simple syrup is an easy way to put a flavorful spin on plain tea, mint juleps, cocktails—even fruit kebabs (page 220). It's easy to make, and the flavor possibilities are endless.

Combine $1/2$ cup water and 1 cup sugar in a small saucepan. Bring to a boil over medium-high heat. Add the flavoring and turn down the heat. Cook, stirring, until all the sugar is dissolved. The longer the syrup boils, the thicker it will be when cool. Strain out the flavorings. Let cool to room temperature. Store in a glass jar in the refrigerator for up to 1 week.

For flavored tea, combine $1/4$ cup of the syrup with 1 cup of tea, adjusting it to your taste.

Some flavoring ideas:

Vanilla bean, lemon, orange, or lime zest, hot chiles, chipotle chiles, coconut, rhubarb, rosemary, lavender, basil, lemon thyme, lemon balm, ginger, cinnamon, cardamom, curry, cloves

Blackberry-Rosemary: use 10 blackberries and the leaves from a 4-inch sprig of fresh rosemary

Ginger-Cardamom: thinly slice a 2-inch piece of fresh ginger and 20 green cardamom pods

MAKE ME HOTTER

- 1 (12-ounce) can shoe peg or other white corn, drained
- 1 (15-ounce) can Bush's black beans, drained
- $1/4$ cup chopped green bell pepper
- 2 tablespoons vegetable oil
- 1 teaspoon salt
- 1 tablespoon red wine vinegar
- $1/4$ cup Herdez salsa verde
- 1 teaspoon ground cumin
- 2 tablespoons chopped cilantro
- Several dashes of hot sauce

Combine all of the ingredients in a medium bowl. Stir gently to combine. Cover and chill. Serve with chips, use as a salad, or use as a topping on fish tacos (next page). Makes $2^{1}/_2$ cups.

GIMMIE S'MORE LOVIN'

A few sweet bites of perfect cookie love!

- 1 roll peanut butter slice-and-bake cookie dough
- 2 marshmallows
- 2 Hershey's Special Dark kisses

Preheat the oven to 350 degrees. Cut four $1/2$-inch slices of the dough. Roll into balls. Transfer to a greased baking sheet.

Use a fork to flatten the dough balls, making a crosshatch pattern.

Use the cap from a 2-liter bottle to cut a circle out of the middle of 2 of the cookies. Bake for 9 to 10 minutes. Remove from the oven and let stand for 1 to 2 minutes. Remove the cut-out cookies from the sheet.

Push the pointy end of each chocolate kiss into a marshmallow. Set on top of the whole cookies. Broil for 1 to 2 minutes until the marshmallows brown. Watch carefully to make sure the cookie doesn't brown too much. (If it is browning too quickly, turn off the heat but leave the pan in the oven so the marshmallows melt.) Remove from the oven.

Top each marshmallow with a cut-out cookie. Press down until the hot marshmallow puffs through the hole. Let cool to firm up. Makes 2 sandwich cookies.

OH BABY CHEESECAKES

The filling keeps in the refrigerator for a few days, so you can bake just enough cheesecake for the two of you anytime you like.

8 ounces cream cheese, softened (the bar type, not the tub type)
1 egg
¼ cup sugar
½ teaspoon vanilla extract
Vanilla wafers
Fruit pie filling, lemon curd, or fresh fruit

Combine the cream cheese, egg, sugar, and vanilla in a food processor or mixer. Process until well blended.

Place paper liners into mini muffin tins. Put a single vanilla wafer into each paper, round side down. Spoon filling mixture over the wafer to fill half the cup. Bake at 350 degrees for 20 minutes. Let the cheesecakes cool. Top with pie filling or lemon curd, or serve with fresh fruit.

SPRING FLING MARTINI

14 mint leaves (reserve two for garnish)
2 tablespoons fresh lime juice
4 ounces cucumber vodka
2 ounces St-Germain elderflower liqueur
Splash of club soda
2 cucumber slices

Muddle 12 mint leaves with the lime juice in a cocktail shaker. Add the vodka, St-Germain, and ice. Shake to blend. Double strain into two martini glasses. Splash with club soda. Garnish each with a mint leaf and a cucumber slice.

ORANGE YOU GOING TO KISS ME

2 ounces Grey Goose® L'Orange Vodka
2 oranges
Diet ginger ale
Limes, strawberries

Add ice cubes to two tall glasses and pour in 2 ounces of vodka. Squeeze the juice of half of a fresh, sliced orange into each glass and top with diet ginger ale. Garnish each with orange slices, a lime wedge, and a strawberry.

MOLL'S HOT & FLIRTY PASTA FOR TWO

I've been preparing this beautiful and super-spicy red, white and green pasta toss for decades, and now family and friends ask for it. It has evolved over the years, but the good news is that there's no right or wrong way to make it. Whatever you have on hand that's fresh and appealing, including different cheeses, fresh or cooked vegetables, tomatoes—the sky is the limit!

The only cooking is boiling the pasta, and the majority of the work is dicing and chopping. Share the work between the two of you, or do it yourself as a true labor of love.

> 3 garlic cloves, minced
> 5 serrano chiles, minced
> 4 red habanero chiles or 1 red bell pepper, minced
> 4 to 6 ounces linguine
> Extra virgin olive oil to taste
> $1/4$ cup freshly grated Parmesan cheese
> Sea salt and freshly ground pepper to taste
> $1/3$ cup pitted kalamata olives, cut into halves
> 2 to 4 fresh basil leaves
> Chopped cooked chicken, optional
> $1/3$ cup freshly grated Parmesan cheese

Combine the garlic, serrano chiles and habanero chiles in a bowl and toss.

Cook the linguine to al dente according to package directions. Drain, then drizzle the hot pasta with a little of the olive oil and sprinkle with the Parmesan cheese. Toss to coat thoroughly.

Divide the pasta between two soup-size bowls. Sprinkle each serving with a tablespoon of the pepper mixture. Season with salt and pepper. Divide the olives between the pasta servings. Top with a basil leaf or two and chicken. Serve with extra Parmesan for sprinkling. Makes 2 servings.

PLEASE BABY PLEASE "MAC & CHEESE"

Rich and luxurious, but also quick and easy. For special occasions or company, spoon the mixture into a greased baking dish. Top with bread crumbs, dot with butter, and broil to brown the crumbs.

1 tablespoon vegetable oil
6 to 8 ounces dried rigatoni
2 cups heavy cream
1 tablespoon chopped fresh rosemary
1 garlic clove, grated or minced
4 ounces herbed goat cheese
1 cup shredded roast chicken
Salt and pepper to taste

Bring a large saucepan of salted water to a boil over high heat. Add the oil and rigatoni. Cook according to package directions, usually 10 to 12 minutes.

Meanwhile, pour the cream into a large saucepan set over medium heat. Add the rosemary and garlic. Bring to a simmer. Watch closely and don't let it boil over. Simmer until the cream is reduced to half its volume.

Stir in the goat cheese and chicken. Cook until the cream coats the back of a spoon.

Drain the pasta well. Add to the sauce. Stir to coat. Cook until heated through and well blended. Serve hot. Makes 2 servings.

SWIMMIN' UPSTREAM

2 garlic cloves, minced
2 tablespoons chopped fresh dill (or 1 tablespoon dried dill)
1 teaspoon freshly grated lemon zest
1/4 teaspoon salt
1/4 teaspoon cayenne pepper
2 tablespoons fresh lemon juice
2 tablespoons coarse-grained mustard such as
   Grey Poupon Harvest Coarse Ground
2 salmon fillets
Lemon wedges and fresh dill for serving

Combine the garlic, dill, lemon zest, salt, cayenne pepper, lemon juice, and mustard in a bowl and mix well. Spread over the salmon.

Coat a grill with nonstick cooking spray, or use a fish grilling pan or basket. Grill with the cover on for 4 to 6 minutes per side until fish flakes easily with a fork. Baste with remaining sauce. Garnish with lemon wedges and fresh dill. Serves 2.

TEMPTING TOMATO

A perfect tomato sandwich is a thing of beauty, and these sandwiches make a perfect appetizer. This recipe puts the components in separate containers. Store them until you are ready to serve. Then assemble when you're ready to eat.

1 medium tomato, thinly sliced
1 thin slice of red onion
Salt and pepper to taste
1 tablespoon tarragon vinegar
1/4 cup best-quality mayonnaise
2 teaspoons lemon juice (optional)
Cayenne pepper to taste
Italian bread rounds
Several shavings of Parmesan cheese

Layer the tomato slices in a plastic container. Top with the onions. Sprinkle with salt, pepper, and vinegar. Seal and refrigerate until needed.

Combine the mayonnaise, lemon juice, and cayenne pepper in a small container. When ready to assemble, pat the tomatoes dry with paper towels. Spread the mayonnaise mixture on the bread. Top with a tomato and a sprinkle of Parmesan cheese. Eat them open-faced or topped with another bread round. Serves 2.

MOLL'S FABULOUS FILETS

Cook four filets and use the extras for Meat Me for Breakfast brunch the next day.

> ³/₄ cup Dale's marinade
> ¹/₂ cup balsamic vinegar
> ¹/₂ cup extra virgin olive oil
> 1 tablespoon minced garlic
> Kosher salt and freshly ground pepper to taste
> 4 slices applewood-smoked bacon
> 4 filets mignons

Combine the marinade, vinegar and oil in a gallon-size ziptop bag or a bowl. Add the garlic, salt, and pepper.

Wrap a piece of bacon around the edge of each filet. Secure with a wooden toothpick. Add the filets to the bag or bowl. Close the bag or cover the bowl. Refrigerate for 30 minutes. Remove from the refrigerator and let stand at room temperature for 15 to 20 minutes. Grill to your preferred doneness. Serves 2 with leftovers.

GETTIN' CHICKEN POT LUCKY

Add a couple of chicken breast halves to the roasting pan when putting it into the oven and you'll have a start on tomorrow night's dinner.

> 2 to 3 tablespoons olive oil
> 1 onion, chopped
> 4 or 5 bacon strips, chopped
> 1 (3-pound) chicken, rinsed, patted dry
> 8 white potatoes, cut into halves or large chunks
> Carrots, cut into chunks, or baby-cut carrots
> 1 cup white wine
> 1 cup chicken broth
> Fresh rosemary sprigs, thyme sprigs, and parsley
> 2 tablespoons butter
> Salt, pepper, and herb seasoning

Heat a large coated or uncoated cast-iron roasting casserole such as Le Creuset. Add the olive oil, onion, and bacon. Cook until the onions are translucent and the bacon is cooked through. Remove from the pot and set aside.

Preheat the oven to 375 degrees. Brown the chicken breast-side down in the hot pot to sear on one side. Turn and sear the other side of the breast. Add more oil to the pot if needed. Turn the chicken breast-side up and sear for 5 minutes. Add the onion and bacon, arranging them around the chicken. Place the potatoes and carrots around the chicken.

Pour in the wine and broth. Stuff the rosemary, thyme, and parsley into the cavity of the chicken. Push butter between the skin and breast meat to keep it moist during cooking. Sprinkle the chicken and vegetables with salt, pepper, and seasoning. Bring the liquid to a boil.

Put the roaster in the oven. Bake for 1 hour 15 minutes. Slice the chicken and serve with the vegetables.

STUFFED WITH AMORÉ

Reserve the artichoke marinade and use it for marinating the chicken.

> 1 (6-ounce) jar marinated artichoke hearts, drained, coarsely chopped
> 2 ounces goat cheese or grated fontina
> 2 tablespoons capers
> 2 tablespoons drained, chopped roasted red pepper
> 2 tablespoons Presto Pesto (page 205)
> ¹/₄ cup coarsely chopped fresh spinach (or 1 tablespoon thawed spinach, squeezed dry)
> 2 (5-ounce) boneless, skinless chicken breasts

MARINADE

Artichoke marinade
Zest and juice of 1 lemon
1 tablespoon chopped fresh rosemary
1 tablespoon honey
Salt to taste
Additional olive oil for sautéing

Combine the artichokes, cheese, pepper, and spinach in a small bowl. Cut a pocket into the side of each chicken breast, working the knife along carefully. Divide the artichoke mixture between the pockets. Press the edge together to enclose the filling.

Combine all of the marinade ingredients in a shallow baking dish. Add the chicken and turn to coat. Cover and refrigerate for 30 minutes. Turn the chicken. Refrigerate for another 30 minutes.

Preheat the oven to 375 degrees. Heat the oil in an ovenproof skillet over medium-high heat. Sauté the chicken for 2 minutes. Turn the chicken. Put the skillet into the oven. Bake for 10 to 15 minutes until chicken is cooked through. Serves 2.

MANGO TANGO FOR TWO

FISH

2 (6-ounce) tilapia fillets (frozen and thawed is fine)
1 tablespoon olive oil
2 tablespoons Caribbean jerk seasoning
¼ teaspoon kosher salt
4 yellow corn tortillas

SALSA

1 cup diced mango
¼ cup minced red onion
2 tablespoons chopped fresh cilantro
1 tablespoon minced Serrano chiles
1 tablespoon olive oil
1 teaspoon minced garlic
¼ teaspoon ground red pepper (cayenne)

Preheat grill to medium-high heat. Brush tilapia evenly with oil; sprinkle both sides with seasoning and salt. Grill 3 minutes per side or until fish is cooked through. Add tortillas to grill; cook 1 minute per side or until lightly charred.

To prepare salsa, combine all ingredients in a small bowl. To make tacos, flake fish and divide evenly between tortillas; top with salsa. Serves 2.

EVENING
recipes for two

MIGHTY APHRODITE'S DINNER FOR TWO

GREEK-STYLE KEBABS

When we're going all-out, we roast a pan of Greek-seasoned potato wedges to go along with the kebabs.

2 steaks or 2 chicken breasts, or 1 of each
Olive oil
Balsamic vinegar
Oregano
Cavender's Greek seasoning
Salt and pepper to taste
1 red onion
1 red bell pepper
1 yellow bell pepper
1 orange bell pepper
1 green bell pepper
2 pita breads
Tzatziki sauce (recipe follows)

If you're using wooden skewers, soak them in water for 30 minutes or more while you prepare and marinate the meat and vegetables.

Cut the meat into bite-size pieces that aren't too thick. Combine the olive oil, vinegar, oregano, Greek seasoning, salt, and pepper in a zip top bag. Add the meat and seal the bag. (Use two bags if you're preparing both chicken and steak.) Refrigerate for at least 1 hour.

Cut the onion into wedges or chunks $^1/_4$- to $^1/_2$-inch wide. Cut the bell peppers into pieces the same size. Combine with olive oil, vinegar mixture, Greek seasoning, salt, and pepper in a bowl. Toss to coat. Cover with foil and refrigerate until ready to cook.

Thread the meat and vegetables on a skewer in this order: onion, red pepper, meat, onion, yellow pepper, meat, onion, orange pepper, meat, onion, green pepper, meat, onion, and any color pepper.

Grill until the meat is cooked through and the vegetables are tender-crisp. Warm 2 pita breads on the grill. Fill with the meat and vegetables. Drizzle with tzatziki sauce. Serves 2.

TZATZIKI SAUCE

1 recipe Lemon Mint Yogurt Dressing (page 206)
1 garlic clove, minced
$^1/_2$ cucumber, grated or finely diced
Salt and Cavender's Greek seasoning to taste

Combine the dressing, garlic, and cucumber. Add salt and Greek seasoning to taste. Refrigerate for an hour or two for flavors to blend. Makes $^2/_3$ cup.

LET'S GET SAUCY

Use fresh ingredients to "doctor up" a jar of pasta sauce, and make your own meatballs for this all-time favorite. Use refrigerated chopped garlic and parsley from a tube (see the note on page 199) to shorten the prep time.

THREE-TOMATO PASTA SAUCE

1 tablespoon finely chopped flat-leaf parsley
1 1/2 teaspoons minced garlic
2 tablespoons olive oil
1 (15-ounce) can petite diced tomatoes, drained
2 cups best-quality prepared pasta sauce
3 tablespoons sun-dried tomato pesto
Salt to taste

MEATBALLS

4 ounces ground round
4 ounces ground Italian sausage, casings removed
1/2 cup bread crumbs
1/2 cup freshly grated Parmesan cheese
2 tablespoons chopped flat-leaf parsley
2 garlic cloves, minced
1 large egg
1/2 teaspoon kosher salt
1/2 teaspoon freshly ground pepper
1/4 teaspoon minced chipotle chile
1/4 teaspoon cayenne pepper
All-purpose flour
1/4 cup olive oil

1/2 pound spaghetti, cooked according to package directions, drained
1/3 cup freshly grated Parmesan cheese

For the sauce, sizzle the parsley and garlic in the olive oil in a medium skillet over medium-high heat. Add the tomatoes, pasta sauce, pesto, and salt. Lower the heat to medium and cook, stirring occasionally, for 20 to 25 minutes until the sauce thickens and the oil begins to separate. (You can make the sauce in advance and refrigerate it for a day or two.)

For the meatballs, put the meats in a mixing bowl, and sprinkle evenly with the bread crumbs, cheese, parsley, and garlic. Beat the

egg with the salt, pepper, chipotle, and cayenne in a small bowl. Pour over the meat. Mix with clean hands or a fork until just blended. Shape the mixture into 1 1/2-inch balls.

Coat the meatballs lightly with flour. Brown in batches in the olive oil in a large skillet over medium-high heat for about 6 minutes, turning to cook all sides. Add the meatballs to the tomato sauce. Cook, stirring gently, for about 30 minutes until meatballs are cooked through.

Combine about 1 cup of the tomato sauce with the pasta. Add the Parmesan cheese. Adjust the seasoning with salt and pepper. Serve the pasta in a big bowl topped with a little more sauce. Add 3 or 4 meatballs to each serving. Makes 3 to 4 servings.

LUSCIOUS LONDON BROIL

Buy a small flank steak for serving two. Leftover meat is ideal for steak and eggs, hash, sandwiches, or burritos.

1/4 cup ketchup
2 tablespoons soy sauce
1/2 cup chopped onion
6 tablespoons water
1/2 tablespoon minced garlic
1 flank steak

Combine the ketchup, soy sauce, onion, water, and garlic in a small bowl. Set the steak in a rectangular glass baking dish. Pour most of the marinade over the steak, reserving a little to baste the steak as it cooks. Cover and refrigerate for at least 8 hours.

Grill or broil the steak to medium or medium-rare—any further cooking can rob flank of its delicious juiciness. Let stand 5 minutes. Set the steak on a cutting board. With a sharp knife held at an angle, cut the steak into slices diagonally.

Plate the lettuce halves (or use bowls if you plan to pile on the ingredients). Spoon dressing over them. Arrange the tomatoes around the lettuce. Sprinkle with bacon bits and onion ring pieces. Serves 2.

ALL STEAMED UP

Make a whole pound of these and you've got enough side dish for two dinners. Just refrigerate and use within two days for the freshest flavor.

> 1 pound fresh green beans
> 1 package dry Good Seasons Italian Dressing mix
> 4 tablespoons butter, cut into bits
> Parmesan cheese

Steam the green beans over or in boiling water for 10 minutes; drain.

Preheat the oven to 350 degrees. Butter a 1-quart casserole dish. Put the green beans in the dish. Sprinkle with the dressing mix. Dot with butter. Top with a generous layer of Parmesan cheese.

Bake for 15 to 20 minutes. Makes 2 to 4 servings.

SPINACH ON THE SIDE

> 2 pounds baby or flat-leaf spinach
> 3 tablespoons extra virgin olive oil
> 1 large garlic clove, sliced
> Kosher salt and freshly ground pepper
> Several slices bacon, cooked and crumbled

A HUNK OF LOVE

Start with a classic lettuce wedge and build layers of flavor with the flavors you like. Make sure the lettuce is very cold for the crunchiest texture.

> 1 head of lettuce, cut in half
> ¼ cup thick-textured, strongly flavored blue cheese dressing such as Marie's
> 1 tomato, chopped
> 4 slices applewood-smoked bacon, crisp-cooked and crumbled
> 8 frozen onion rings, baked or fried until very crisp, chopped

Trim the stems of the leaves and then wash the leaves thoroughly. Shake or pat dry, leaving a little water on the leaves.

Combine olive oil and garlic in large skillet. Cook over medium heat until the garlic begins to change color. Add the spinach, then salt lightly. Cover the pan. Cook until some of the spinach wilts. Stir to move the cooked spinach to the edge of the pan. Cook until all the spinach is wilted, stirring occasionally. Drain the excess liquid. Add crumbled bacon and cook for 1 to 3 minutes longer. Season with salt and pepper. Serves 2.

TEASE ME BROCCOLINI

Cannellini beans have a creamy texture and a refined, slightly sweet taste that contrasts with broccolini's sharp, bitter flavor. Add 1 pound of sweet Italian sausage and a little cooked pasta for an easy skillet supper.

    2 garlic cloves, minced
    1/2 cup finely chopped yellow onion
    3 tablespoons olive oil
    Salt and red pepper flakes to taste
    1/2 bunch broccolini, coarsely chopped, tough stems removed
    1/4 cup water
    1 tablespoon honey
    1 cup cooked cannellini beans
    2 tablespoons white wine vinegar
    3 tablespoons golden raisins
    3 tablespoons pine nuts

Sauté the garlic and onion in the olive oil in a large skillet over medium heat until the onion is translucent. Add the salt and pepper flakes. Add the broccolini. Cook until the broccolini turns bright green and begins to wilt. Add the water and honey. Cook for 10 minutes until the broccolini is tender. Stir in the beans, vinegar, and raisins. Heat through. Top with pine nuts. Serves 2.

WHISPER TO ME

Each bite is a refreshing combination of crisp sweet apple, a whisper of licorice, and sunny lemon.

    Juice of 1 lemon
    2 tablespoons best-quality olive oil
    1/2 teaspoon Dijon mustard
    1/4 teaspoon salt
    Pepper to taste
    A touch of honey (optional)
    1 small, sweet, crisp apple, quartered
    1/2 small fennel bulb
    Fennel fronds
    Parmesan shavings (optional)

Combine the lemon juice, olive oil, mustard, salt, pepper, and honey in a medium bowl and mix well. Use a mandoline or slicer to shave the apple and fennel into very thin slices. Add to the dressing and toss to coat. Top with Parmesan, if desired. Serves 2.

SWEET STICKS

Cubes of pineapple, mango, apple, plum, peach, and strawberry
Ginger-Cardamom Simple Syrup (page 210)

Soak 2 wooden grill skewers in water for 20 to 30 minutes to prevent burning.

Thread the cubed fruits alternately onto the skewers, leaving a little space between each piece to allow for flavorful browning. Use a pastry or marinade brush to paint the kebab on all sides with the glaze. Grill on medium-low heat for about 5 minutes, turning occasionally, until kebobs have grill marks on all sides. Brush again with syrup before serving. Serves 2.

DRIPPING IN CHOCOLATE

Push a toothpick into the stem end of the strawberry for a "handle" for easy dipping.

6 strawberries
3 amaretti cookies
Dark melting chocolate

Wash and dry the strawberries. Crush the amaretti cookies to crumbs in a plastic bag with a rolling pin or in a food processor. Pour onto a shallow plate.

Melt the chocolate in a double boiler over simmering water, stirring until smooth. (Or melt in a microwave at 50 percent power for 90 seconds, then stir. Heat in 10-second intervals until melted.)

Dip the strawberries into the chocolate. Quickly roll in amaretti crumbs. Makes 6 strawberries.

KISS ME GINGERLY

With ice cream, it's dessert. Without the ice cream, it's a deliciously different fruit side dish for Thai or Indian meals.

1 tablespoon butter, softened
1 tablespoon brown sugar
Pinch of cloves
1/2 teaspoon grated fresh ginger
1 teaspoon lime juice
2 teaspoons orange juice
2 bananas, peels on, cut into halves lengthwise

Preheat the oven or grill to 375 degrees. Beat the butter with the sugar, cloves, ginger, lime juice, and orange juice. Put the banana halves in a greased baking dish.

Spread the butter mixture over the bananas. Bake or grill for 10 minutes until the bananas are tender. Serve on their own or over coconut ice cream. Serves 2.

BABY CAKES

- 1 cup all purpose flour
- 2 tablespoons granulated sugar
- 2 teaspoons baking powder
- 1 teaspoon lemon zest
- 1/4 teaspoon salt
- 2 tablespoons cold butter, cut into small pieces
- 2 tablespoons heavy cream
- 1 large egg, lightly beaten
- 1/4 cup blueberries
- 1 1/2 cups quartered strawberries
- 2 tablespoons sugar
- 1/2 cup frozen whipped topping, thawed

Preheat oven to 475 degrees. Combine flour, sugar, powder, zest, and salt in a large bowl. Cut in butter with pastry blender or 2 knives until mixture resembles coarse meal. Stir in cream and egg, stirring just until moist. Stir in blueberries. Scoop mixture into 2 shortcakes on a parchment-lined baking sheet. Bake for 22–25 minutes or until browned on top. Remove from oven; let cool completely.

Combine strawberries and sugar in a small bowl; let stand 15 minutes or until syrupy. To assemble shortcakes, cut in half; top with macerated strawberries and whipped topping. Garnish with mint leaves, if desired. Serves 2.

SHOTS OF CHOCOLATE DESIRE

- 2 1/2 ounces vodka, chilled
- 2 ounces Frangelico, chilled

Shake the vodka and Frangelico. Chill in the freezer, if you like. Drink ice cold in shot glasses or cordial glasses. Alternatively, serve in rock glasses with sugared rims. Serves 2.

CHILE-INFUSED LIQUOR

Serve as "hot shots" or use in one of the cocktail recipes that follow. Straining out the chiles is easier if you infuse the mixture in a 1-quart canning jar.

6 red serrano chiles
2 green serrano chiles
1 liter vodka or tequila

Wash all the chiles. Trim the stems, split open, and deseed 3 red chiles and 1 green chile. Drop into the bottle of liquor. Let steep in a dark spot, shaking occasionally, for 48 hours. Strain out the chiles. Add 3 whole red and 1 whole green chile. These won't add heat, just a great look—and they warn people that this is hot stuff!

Also, instead of chili peppers try infusing liquors with fresh fruits or herbs.

SPANK IT & SHAKE IT MARTINI

6 ounces chile-infused vodka
1 ounce dry vermouth
Dash of Peychaud bitters
2 hot pickled olives or 2 small pickled okra

Combine the vodka, vermouth, and bitters with ice in a cocktail shaker. Shake hard. Strain into 2 martini glasses. Drop an olive into each drink. Serves 2.

HOT UNDER THE COLLAR

½ cup fresh lime juice
2 to 4 ounces chile-infused tequila
1 ounce Grand Marnier or Triple Sec
2 lime wedges
Salt

Combine the lime juice, tequila, and Triple Sec in a shaker. Rub a lime wedge around the rims of 2 margarita glasses. Dip the rims into salt. Fill with ice. Pour the drink over the ice. Serves 2.

BEND & SNAP

- Lemon wedge
- Granulated sugar
- 3 ounces Calvados or other apple brandy
- 1 ounce ginger liqueur
- 2 tablespoons fresh lemon juice
- Crystallized ginger or lemon twist for garnish

Run a lemon wedge around the rims of 2 small martini glasses. Spread the sugar on a plate. Dip the rims of the glasses in sugar. Combine the Calvados, liqueur and lemon juice in a shaker with ice. Shake for 10 seconds. Strain into the martini glasses. Garnish with a piece of crystallized ginger or a sliver of lemon. Serves 2.

PUCKER UP

- 3 ounces tea-flavored vodka
- 2/3 cup fresh lemon juice (about 2 lemons)
- 1/3 cup simple syrup or flavored syrup (page 210)
- Lemon twist

Shake or stir together the vodka, lemon juice, and simple syrup. Adjust proportions to taste. Serve over ice in a tall glass. Garnish with a twist. Serves 2.

SEDUCTION IN A GLASS

Scotch separates the real men from the boys. You won't find many recipes for Scotch cocktails as it is intended to be savored slowly over ice. Keeping it super simple is all the seduction you need.

- Rocks glass
- Ice
- 3 ounces of your partner's favorite Scotch
- Seductive CD of your choice

Pour Scotch over ice in just the right rocks glass. Add garnish *only* if your partner prefers it that way. Turn on the music. Cozy up to your partner with your favorite cocktail and enjoy the evening together.

Setting up your own seductive bar with all your favorites for two can create the perfect escape without actually going anywhere. Whether you prefer Jack & Coke, an ice-cold beer, wine or simply sparking water in a beautiful glass, tailor your seductive bar for two just the way you like it.   —*Moll*

ESSENTIAL HERBS

DAZZLE THE SENSES

A. Basil—Sweetly fragrant and not too picky about where it grows, basil is a key flavor note in cuisines as diverse as Thai and Italian.

B. Parsley—Just a bit of chopped parsley adds a fresh, celery-like flavor to sauces, salads, and soups.

C. Chives—Snip into potatoes, cream soups, eggs, and salads for a touch of pungent onion flavor and pretty green speckles.

D. Thyme—Tiny thyme leaves hold a powerful earthy fragrance that blends beautifully in long-cooked dishes like beans and stews.

E. Sage—Southwestern dishes come alive with the addition of a sage leaf or two.

F. Mint—The tingly, slightly numbing property of mint makes it perfect for livening up foods and drinks.

G. Rosemary—Perfumey and distinctive, rosemary is a natural partner for chicken.

H. Oregano—Oregano is the signature flavor in Italian red tomato sauce and is indispensible for pizza.

I. Dill and fennel—These feathery fronds are full of perfumey flavors. Dill is grassy and lemony, and fennel is licorice flavored.

J. Tarragon—The delicate licorice flavor of tarragon is a quintessentially French addition to chicken dishes.

K. Cilantro/coriander—This distinctive green leaf gives Thai, Vietnamese, and Mexican food a sharp, slightly soapy punch.

FOODS OF LOVE

TASTES OF DESIRE

Many herbs, spices and foods contain natural aphrodisiacs or sexual enhancing characteristics. The list is endless, but here are few to get you started.

SAFFRON

Just a small amount of saffron can increase sex drive. It has antioxidant qualities, and supplies selenium, zinc, potassium, and magnesium. Try making some saffron brown rice.

CURRY

It has been found that curry can increase the sex drive in men with low libido.

FENNEL

The ancient Egyptians used fennel to boost women's libidos, and it turns out there is a good reason it worked. Fennel contains chemicals that might increase sex drive.

CLOVES

Cloves are a warming and sweet spice that have been shown to increase blood flow and body temperature. This spice also increases energy, sweetens your breath, and is a powerful sexual attractant.

GARLIC

Most people avoid garlic because they don't want to kill the mood with smelly breath on a romantic night. However, the high levels of allicin in garlic improves blood flow to your sexual organs— a definite turn on.

VANILLA

The taste or smell of vanilla is known as the most sexually arousing scent to men.

WILD ROSE

An erotic stimulant especially for females; its rose petals are used in tea and the oil of the rose is used in perfume.

NUTMEG

Nutmeg is a sweetly scented spice and a very popular libido booster in many cultures. In Africa it has even been called "Viagra for women." Nutmeg has been found to increase sexual behavior.

MUSTARD

The spicy flavor of mustard increases blood flow, stimulating the sexual glands. This causes an increase in adrenalin, and sexual desire. The mustard plant promotes fertility and it has been said that for this reason monks were forbidden to eat it.

BASIL

The stimulating scent of basil is known to increase sex drive. It has been said that eating one leaf a day will insure an exciting sex life.

HONEY

Honey is associated with love and sex in both the Bible and the Karma Sutra. It's known to boost stamina in men. Most potent are honeys from bees that gather nectar from aphrodisiac flowers such as jasmine, orchids, or marjoram.

PINEAPPLE

Use fresh pineapple juice as an invigorator—eat with chili powder, or mix with honey and rum to promote sexual desire.

GINGKO

Grilled gingko seeds are very beneficial in bringing power to the lower abdomin area in men.

HORSERADISH

Popular for renewing strength after sexual exhaustion, horseradish, like other bold spices, instigates love.

SWEET POTATO

This veggie is a passion ignitor and when consumed on a regular basis can be a stimulant for women.

YLANG-YLANG

This oil is known to increase eroticism and can be used internally or externally. It is found in many body lotions and candles.

ESSENTIAL SPICES

Coriander—Works well with both sweet and savory foods. Grind and add to cookies, or coat chicken before grilling.

Cinnamon—Used since ancient times, cinnamon makes a home smell homey. Use it with abandon in baked goods. Plenty of long-simmered meats benefit from a cinnamon stick in the pot.

Cumin—From the Southwest to the Middle East, cumin arouses appetites with its tantalizing fragrance.

Paprika—Deep red paprika promises (and delivers) a rich pepper flavor. It's common in Spanish and Hungarian foods.

Fennel—Small, striped seed with a big licorice flavor that's at home in Italian and Scandinavian food and is wonderful with fish.

Chili powder—Heats up any dish with a little ground fire. The mixture typically includes cumin, oregano, and sometimes garlic.

Nutmeg—Warm, sweet flavor and that goes naturally with autumn foods like winter squash, sweet potatoes, carrots, custard, raisins, and other fruit.

FENNEL · CUMIN · PEPPER

CINNAMON · PAPRIKA · NUTMEG

CHILI POWDER · SALT · CORIANDER

Kosher salt—Coarse, flat grain that adds crunch as well as seasoning. Kosher salt makes the best rub for grilled meat.

Black pepper—Good quality peppercorns have just enough bite to get your attention, and more fragrance than heat.

Fun Fact: Herbs and spices are as personal as choosing scents and flavors that you love.

Don't buy pre-filled spice racks. Purchase your essentials separately to have on hand and then buy what you're drawn to and what speaks to all of your senses.

Remember that spices have about a six-month shelf life.

CAYENNE PEPPER CARDAMOM COCOA TURMERIC

HOT AND TANGY, THIS MIX CAPTURES THE ESSENCE OF MOLL'S FAVORITE TASTES!

CHILI PEPPERS SUMAC GINGER CHIPOTLE

Cayenne Pepper—A basic for the seductive kitchen, cayenne stimulates circulation and its effects mimic the physiological response the body has during sex.

Cardamom—Cooked with meats, ground for cookies, steeped with tea, or simmered with rice, cardamom fills the kitchen with a scent like no other.

It's used in some locales as a treatment for impotence.

Chocolate (cocoa powder)—The ultimate caress for the seductive palate, chocolate contains serotonin and phenylethlyamine, two "feel good" chemicals.

Turmeric—Adds an appealing deep yellow color and a slightly warm, peppery flavor. Ideal for fish, rice, and baked macaroni and cheese.

Chili peppers—Fresh or dried, these are indispensible for imparting the maximum flavor to meals.

Sumac—Shake this tangy, crunchy topping on Greek and Middle Eastern dishes, including rice, chicken, and fish.

Ginger—Fresh and grated or dried and ground, this globally-beloved spice heats up baked goods, meats, even ice cream, and stimulates circulation.

Chipotle—This dark pepper spice adds a rich, smoky flavor that will kick up any dish without too much heat.

EVERYDAY TO GOURMET

BREAKFAST

- Cheese blintzes, found in the frozen food section, are great for an inpromtu morning in bed. Prepare as indicated. Sprinkle powdered sugar and garnish with fruit, jam, and sour cream.
- Put a fresh frame around fried eggs: cut four 1-inch-high rings of red bell pepper. Put them into a buttered skillet. Break an egg into each ring and fry to desired doneness. Or scramble the egg with herbs and pour into "pepper frames" in a skillet.
- Dessert for breakfast! Spread ice cream between two toasted mini waffles. Add a swipe of peanut butter or marshmallow crème.

APPETIZERS AND SNACKS

- Keep the pantry stocked with cocktail snacks and you're always ready for entertaining, even if it's just the two of you.
- Cheese straws, Wheat Thins, olives, pickled okra, and spicy nut mix can all be placed in pretty bowls and in front of guests in minutes.
- Keep a bar of cream cheese in the refrigerator and a jar of red bell pepper Ancho Chili Jam in the pantry for an instant appetizer. Plate the cream cheese, then spoon or pour on the pepper jelly. Serve with melba toast or crackers.
- At the top of your party pantry list, keep jars of sun-dried tomato tapenade, tomato bruschetta, and an array of olives. Pair them with olives and mozzarella for a bruschetta topper.
- You'll keep finding uses for a jar of olive tapenade, too. Use it on sandwiches, as a pizza topping, or for bruschetta. Add a spoonful to red sauce for pasta. Combine with caramelized onions as a topping for baked fish. Roll with salami in flatbread and slice into pinwheels.

LUNCH AND DINNER

- Frozen artichoke hearts are a must in my kitchen. They're great as a quick stuffing for chicken or tossed with pasta, peppers, and Italian sausage. For a rustic Italian dip, cook them with garlic, olive oil, and cream. Purée, then serve with fresh vegetables and rustic bread.

- Frozen spinach artichoke dip is another product you'll use over and over. Thaw and use it as a sauce for chicken breasts or pork chops. Top baked potatoes with it. Stuff it into cored, deseeded tomatoes and bake until hot.

- Vegetarian refried beans are simple to transform into a creamy bean soup with just broth and milk, plus plenty of spicy seasonings. Serve with Tostitos tortilla chips.

- To spice up a can of Campbell's Tomato Soup, substitute a can of original V8 for water. Flavor with Worcestershire sauce and Tabasco. Serve hot with grated cheddar cheese and bacon bits.

- Do the same with prepared refrigerated mashed potatoes—just add broth, half-and-half or milk, and some fresh chives for creamy potato soup.

- Black bean-and-rice mix cooks in about 20 minutes for a light meal or side dish that's a change of pace. Fluff it and cool slightly, then use it to stuff burritos. Or turn it into a salad with chopped parsley, celery, green onion and vinaigrette.

- More and more food companies offer pre-packaged pulled pork that's almost as good as your local barbecue joint. Just heat it up and finish with a drizzle of your favorite barbecue sauce. Splurge on best-quality buns, or use the barbecue on top of a salad.

- Have you discovered Kraft's "Fresh Take" cheese and bread crumb mixtures? They're simply amazing. Use them to bread fish, chicken, cutlets, or croquettes. Use the mixture to stuff pork chops or roll into flattened chicken breasts. Stir them into meatloaf, stuff into mushroom caps, or sprinkle them onto casseroles or baked vegetables for au gratin.

- Broccoli slaw utilizes the stalks, which are full of fiber and nutrients. Add a gingery dressing and some wasabi almonds for a quick side dish. They're ideal for stir-fry, or for simmering in chicken and rice soup for a homemade taste.

- Make twice-baked potatoes with a little something extra. Scoop out the flesh and combine with an all-natural French onion or green onion dip. Stuff the potatoes, top with cheese and bake until hot.

SWEET FINALES

- Slip into some seductive chocolate late at night. Cut slices of frozen double chocolate pound cake into bite-size squares. Set them in miniature cupcake liner papers. Arrange on a silver tray or in a silver candy dish. Add miniature frozen chocolate eclairs, Twix ice cream bar minis, and frozen peppermint patty ice cream bites. Stash the tray in the freezer.

- Pre-made crepes found in the refrigerator section are perfect to have on hand for creating decadent desserts in no time. Mix two ounces of Cool Whip with two vanilla pudding cups and fill crepes. Top with fresh fruit and drizzle with chocolate syrup.

WARDROBE FOR THE TABLE

Think of your tableware as fashion for the table. Each tablescape design is an expression of your individual style. You would change your table décor to fit the occasion, just as you would change your outfit. As with any wardrobe, mix and match your pieces to create new, interesting, and unique designs.

Collecting a table or tray wardrobe isn't difficult and doesn't need to be expensive. Look for pieces you love in pairs and don't be afraid to mix them. Assemble vintage with modern, high-end selections with inexpensive pieces, and contrast colors with textures. Add an eclectic mix of interesting accessories and one-of-a-kind finds.

DINNERWARE

Your dinnerware collection can include a menagerie of items—everything from fine china and bone china to stoneware and hand-made pottery, including dining and serving pieces. Adding a charger to your setting will add more interest to your table.

FLATWARE

Flatware is made from many different metals: sterling silver, silver plate, and stainless steel. Some even have handles made out of natural materials such as bone, stone, and wood. Select everyday utensils that are comfortable in your hand and are easy to maintain; but most importantly, collect the silverware that you love.

GLASSWARE AND STEMWARE

Glassware and stemware are available in vibrant colors, subtle pastels, smoky tints, etched finishes, and exquisite crystal. Once you've put together your basic crystal collection, begin collecting many other unusual styles and mix them to create an interesting combination of shapes and sizes.

LINENS

Layer placemats, tablecloths, runners, and antique linens. Use contrasting colors and textures to add your own style to the tablescape.

LIGHTING

Set the mood of your table with your selection of lighting. Having your lights on dimmer switches is ideal, but remember to include candlelight. Enhance your table with candles in glass hurricane lanterns. Scatter glass votives throughout to create shimmering light.

TABLE SETTING—FORMAL

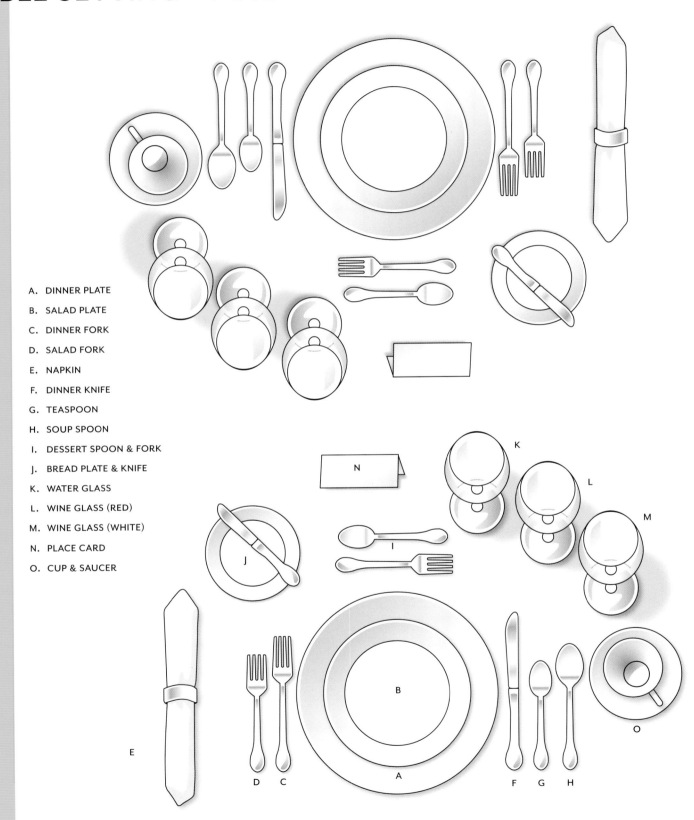

A. DINNER PLATE

B. SALAD PLATE

C. DINNER FORK

D. SALAD FORK

E. NAPKIN

F. DINNER KNIFE

G. TEASPOON

H. SOUP SPOON

I. DESSERT SPOON & FORK

J. BREAD PLATE & KNIFE

K. WATER GLASS

L. WINE GLASS (RED)

M. WINE GLASS (WHITE)

N. PLACE CARD

O. CUP & SAUCER

A. DINNER PLATE

B. NAPKIN

C. DINNER FORK

D. SALAD FORK

F. DINNER KNIFE

G. TEASPOON

H. SOUP SPOON

K. WATER GLASS

L. WINE GLASS

STEMWARE

COCKTAIL

GLASSES

HIGH BALL

ROCKS

SHOT

MARTINI/COCKTAIL

COLLINS

MARGARITA

IRISH COFFEE

BEER

GLASSES

MUG

PILSNER

STEMWARE

WHITE WINE

RED WINE

CLARET WINE

WATER GOBLET

CORDIAL

COUPE/SAUCER

TULIP

TRUMPET FLUTE

FLUTE

INDEX

ORANGE COVER TABLE:
Juliska—"octavia" glasses • **Caspari**—placemats • **Herend**—charger • **Alberto Pinto**—dinner plates • **Kim Seybert**—"Ombre" napkins, "Rock Arch" napkin rings • **Dransfield & Ross**—"Linen Weave Edge" napkins • **Baccarat**—bowls • **John Derian**—decoupage heart plate

LUSCIOUS IN LAVENDER:
Jan Barboglio—"Nickle Corazon Hand Pisapapel" heart • **Jay Strongwater**—"Susanna" Boxwood Pig Figurine • **L'objet**—picture frame/place card holder • **Merletto**—Antique White Dinnerware, dinner plate • **Arte Italica**—tesoro beaded charger • **Kim Seybert**—placemat, napkins, napkin rings • **Bella Note**—lace tablecloth • **Ercole**—mosaic glass bowl • **Christopher Guy**—chairs • **Dransfield & Ross**—ostrich feather pillow • **Lafco**—candle • **Theresienthal**—Kurbistiasche bottle, fern bowl • lavender tablecloth—remnant fabric from craft store • lace tablecloth overlay—family heirloom

SENSUAL SEA ESCAPE:
L'objet—gold bowl • **Royal Crown Derby**—"Red Aves" salad plate • **Herend**—"Chinese Boquet" plate • **Dransfield & Ross**—"Linen wave edge" napkins • **Arte Italia**—glassware • top tablecloth, shawl • middle tablecloth, antique store • **Recollections, Santa Fe, NM**—bottom tablecloth • **Dransfield & Ross**—Cloisonne Lobster napkin rings

ARTICHOKE AFFAIR:
Jars—"Tourron" eggplant dinnerware • **Le Jacquard Francais**—"Bosphore" purple table linens • tablecloth overlay—flea market find • **Anali**—embroidered artichoke linen hand towel • **Hobby Lobby**—glass bowl/flower container • **Anali**—embroidered artichoke linen hand towel • **Bennett Galleries**—nested egg condiment dish • **Roost**—amethyst salt & pepper shaker

FRESH AND FLIRTY PASTA:
Pier 1 Imports—wine glasses • **Alex Marshal**—round plates • **Anichini**—napkins • **Bennett Galleries**—wine rack table • **Alain Saint Joanis**—Griffe flatware

SAVORY SUNRISE:
Hermés—"Balcon Du Guadalquivir" china • **Juan De Chrome**—Berlin silver-plate flatware • **Kim Seybert**—napkins • **Linen Way**—tea towels • **The Ann Lawrence Collection**—antique lace piece as table overlay • **Kohl's**—white china (inset picture)

PASSIONATE PICNIC:
Jan Barboglio—"San Sergio d'piso" Candelabra, chalice, fruit bowl, "Ballin" iron bead tray, "vessel d'lux" glass bowls • **Ralph Lauren**—leather tray, "Indian Cove Lodge Stool" • **Two Girls in Avignon**—velvet trimmed linens • **Bella Notte**—bolster pillow • **Anichini**—fringe towels • **Ann Gish**—"crushed taffeta" napkins

HOT DIGGITY DOG:
Pier 1 Imports—food trays, red and white ant platter, mustard and ketchup bottles, napkins • **Vietri**—dishes • **Dransfield & Ross**—butterfly napkin rings • **World Market**—silverware • tablecloth—Santa Fe flea market

SUSHI SENSATION:
Pier 1 Imports—plates, bowls, place mats, chopsticks sets, sake set, candle votives, napkins • **Bodrum**—coral napkin ring • tablecloth—Moll's personal hand knit shawl

SANTA FE SEDUCTION:
Pier 1 Imports—floor mat, tablecloth, place mats, plates, bowls, napkins, napkin rings • **TJ Maxx**—flatware • **The Ann Lawrence Collection**—pillows

TEA FOR TWO:
Pier 1 Imports—glasses, beverage carafe • **Jan Barboglio**—candle votive • **Dransfield & Ross**—butterfly napkin rings • **Bennett Galleries**—rocking chairs, table, pillows, rug

RED HOT VALENTINE:
Baccarat—candlesticks • **St. Louis**—crystal • **Hobby Lobby**—King & Queen of Hearts pillows, glitter hearts • **TJ Maxx**—red glasses • **Anichini**—hand towels • red tablecloth—craft store fabric by the yard • lace tablecloth overlay—family heirloom

DELECTABLE DESSERTS:
Juliska—"Harriet" covered urn, "Ursula" teacake stand, decanter • **Annieglass**—gold ruffle cake stand • **Ercole**—glass candle votive • **Hobby Lobby**—flower vases • **TJ Maxx**—cupcake stand

HOLIDAY ELEGANCE:
JL Coquet—"Hemisphere" charger, gold-striped dinner plate, dessert plate, gold-striped teacup, "Samoa" teacup • **Herend**—"Gwendolyn" white dinner plate • **Juliska**—"Graham" goblet • **Dransfield & Ross**—napkins • **Vietri**—"Aladdin" flatware • **Kim Seybert**—placemat • **Michael's**—ornaments, ribbons, and wrapping

CREDITS

HANUKKAH NIGHTCAP:
Hermés—"Bleus d'Ailleurs" china • **Matteo**—"Folk" table linen • **A.C. Moore**—gift-wrap, napkin ring ornaments • **Bennett Galleries**—wine goblets

HOLIDAY GIVING TREE:
Baccarat—ice bucket and champagne flutes • **Neiman Marcus**—candle votives

PACKING YOUR PICNIC (p. 90):
World Market—picnic basket • **Walmart**—glass jars

WARDROBE FOR YOUR TABLE (p. 230):
ZGallerie—dishes, tray, placemat, napkins, napkin rings • **Frette**—bedding

Moll Anderson, **Moll Anderson Productions** in conjunction with Matthew Wiseman, **RedManGroup**—p. 203: Red Hot Bloody Mary • p.221: Pucker Up • p.222: Shots of Desire

Bennett Galleries
5308 Kingston Pike
Knoxville, TN 37919
865.584.6791
www.bennettgalleries.com

Cielo Tabletop
316 S. Guadalupe Street
Santa Fe, NM 87501
505.992.1960
www.cielohome.com

Gift & Gourmet Interiors
5508 Kingston Pike
Knoxville, TN 37919
865.212.5639
info@gg-interiors.com

Neiman Marcus—www.neimanmarcus.com

Pier 1 Imports—www.pier1.com

Z Gallerie—www.zgallerie.com

ReCreations Furniture, Nashville, TN—holiday decorations

www.orientaltrading.com

PHOTOGRAPHY | CREDITS

beall + thomas Photography: 9, 16 (top & bottom left side), 22, 24, 26-30, 36, 38, 39-41, 75 (inset), 84-86, 90, 132 (left side & right side top & bottom), 138-140, 142, 144, 146-150, 152, 153 (right), 154, 156-160, 162-164, 166-170, 176-178, 180, 182-186, 188-190, 198 (top left), 199-201, 207, 208, 215, 216, 218, 219, 221, 222, 223 (top right), 224, 226, 227, 230, endsheets, back cover

DeLong Photography: Cover, 239

Eric Anderson Photography: 12, 16 (center), 20-21, 32-33, 34, 42, 82, 83, 88, 89, 132 (center), 136, 137, 153 (left)

John Hall Photography: 16 (top & bottom right), 44-45, 46, 48, 50-54, 56-58, 60, 62, 63, 64-66, 68-70, 72, 74-76, 78, 92-96, 98, 99, 100, 102-106, 109, 112-116, 118-120, 122, 123, 124-126, 128,130, 194, 212

Michael Gomez Photography: 108

iStock: 62, 110, 129, 132 (right side center), 172, 174, 192, 196, 197, 198 (bottom right), 202-204, 211, 220, 223 (bottom left), 228

FASHION

Cover: **LaPerla**—pajamas • page 12: **Erdem**—dress • page 16: **Oscar de la Renta**—dress • page 20: **Prada**—dress • page 32: **Carolina Herrera** • page 78: **Michael Kors**—dress • page 82: Zac Posen—dress • page 108: **www.oriental-clothing.com**—dress • page 132: **Jason Wu**—dress • page 137: **Oscar de la Renta**—dress, **Christian Louboutin**—shoes • page 153: **Oscar de la Renta**—dress • Back Inside Cover: **Dior**—dress, shoes

MOLL ANDERSON

Moll Anderson is an accomplished interior designer and lifestyle expert who infused the interior design world with a fresh new way of thinking. Her first book, *Change Your Home, Change Your Life* (Cool Springs Press, 2006), inspired readers beyond the basics of paint and fabric and showed them that making small, inexpensive changes both in their homes and lifestyles is the most important investment they will make. More than simple design advice, it was commonsense with a kick of encouragement. Moll's five must-haves, paint, lighting, music, flowers, and fabric, were her simple jump-start plan to inspire people to get out of a rut and on their way to living a better life.

Moll followed the success of her first book with *The Seductive Home*™ *Limited Edition* in November 2011. The beautiful coffee table book is filled with images of elegant, seductive spaces and creative entertaining options, encouraging readers to create an intimate space of their own, one that seduces them and their guests every time they walk through the door. Moll shared her inspiration and her essential keys for creating a welcoming, seductive home in the trade edition of *The Seductive Home*™ (February 2012), where readers learn to add decadent details™ and a touch of romance to their homes.

Moll's career has been filled with many professional achievements and from winning an Emmy for her work as an entertainment reporter, being chosen as one of Donna Karan's *Women Who Inspire,* to bringing her design prowess and no-nonsense relationship advice to such television shows as *Access Hollywood Live* (June 2012), *The Talk* (spring 2012), *The Doctors* (spring 2012), *Good Morning America, The Today Show, Dr. Phil,* Style Network's *"Look for Less: Home Edition,"* and HGTV's *"Hot Trends in Outdoor Entertaining."* She has been featured in both national publications, such as *InStyle, Cosmopolitan, and USA Today,* and regional publications, such as *Elegant Living Magazine, Angeleno Magazine,* and *Arizona Foothills Magazine.* Moll can now be heard every Saturday at 2 PST/5 EST on XMTalk 168 satellite radio. On *The Moll Anderson Show,* Moll gives real-life advice, shares personal experiences, chats with exciting guests, and talks all things seduction! Moll pens a monthly column for *Nashville Lifestyles* and publishes a weekly life and style blog for Magazines.com and on her website at MollAnderson.com. Moll also communicates to her Twitter followers @MollAnderson and on Facebook and Pinterest.